MW00329353

Loving Mountains,
Loving Men

OHIO UNIVERSITY PRESS SERIES IN
ETHNICITY AND GENDER IN APPALACHIA

Series Editor: Lynda Ann Ewen

Memphis Tennessee Garrison: The Remarkable Story of a Black Appalachian Woman,
edited by Ancella R. Bickley and Lynda Ann Ewen

The Tangled Roots of Feminism, Environmentalism, and Appalachian Literature,
by Elizabeth S. D. Engelhardt

Red, White, Black, and Blue: A Dual Memoir of Race and Class in Appalachia,
by William M. Drennen Jr. and Kojo (William T.) Jones Jr.,
edited by Dolores M. Johnson

Beyond Hill and Hollow: Original Readings in Appalachian Women's Studies,
edited by Elizabeth S. D. Engelhardt

Loving Mountains, Loving Men,
by Jeff Mann

Loving Mountains, Loving Men

Jeff Mann

Ohio University Press
Athens

Ohio University Press, Athens, Ohio 45701
www.ohio.edu/oupress
© 2005 by Ohio University Press
Printed in the United States of America
All rights reserved
Ohio University Press books are printed on acid-free paper ∞ ™

12 11 10 09 08 07 06 05   5 4 3 2 1

Title page photograph of Blue Ridge Mountains by Jerome L. Cosyn

Library of Congress Cataloging-in-Publication Data
Loving mountains, loving men / Jeff Mann.
    p. cm. — (Ohio University Press series in ethnicity and gender in Appalachia)
    ISBN 0-8214-1649-9 (acid-free paper) — ISBN 0-8214-1650-2 (pbk. : acid-free paper)
    1. Mann, Jeff. 2. Mann, Jeff—Childhood and youth. 3. Mann, Jeff—Homes and haunts—
West Virginia. 4. Mountain life—Appalachian Region, Southern. 5. Poets, American—20th
century—Biography. 6. College teachers—United States—Biography. 7. Appalachian Region,
Southern—Biography. 8. West Viginia—Social life and customs. 9. Gay men—United
States—Biography. 10. Gay youth—West Virginia. I. Title. II. Series.
    PS3563.A53614Z468 2005
    811'.54—dc22

                                                                        2005010299

For my father, Perry Mann, and my sister, Amy Mann
For John Ross, Cynthia Burack, and Laree Martin
For Jo Davison and Patricia Nell Warren

In memory of my mother, Clara Frances McCormick Mann;
my grandmother, Pauline Ferrell White;
and my aunt, Doris Mann Roberts

Contents

Plates

Preface
Constructing Heaven

Do I contradict myself?
Very well then I contradict myself,
(I am large, I contain multitudes.)

——*"Song of Myself," Walt Whitman*

I dress quietly, not wanting to wake my partner, John. Leaving the cabin, I head for the guest house, ready for some coffee and some time alone to write. Along the path, across the fence, the horses stand, enjoying the cool of the morning, the absence of biting flies. Dew drips from the pine needles, and thistles edge the pasture, small explosions of lavender, reminding me of Scotland, where my mother's family came from: beautiful, prickly blooms. Stubborn, able to survive the harshest landscapes. An endurance I admire.

In the downstairs breakfast room, I pour coffee, listening to the music in the kitchen, where the guest house owners are preparing a big country breakfast, what smells like pancakes and sausage. Out on the upstairs screened-in porch, there is no music, only the sound of a crow, the hum of pool machinery. From this perspective, I can watch mist rise from the coves of the Potomac Highlands, hear a flicker rapping somewhere, watch a hummingbird fly by. Here I can muse on heaven.

In *Storming Heaven* by Denise Giardina, one of my favorite authors, the character Carrie Bishop states, "Heaven is where everyone you love is all in one place." I think of that quotation when John and I take one of our too-infrequent trips back to my hometown of Hinton, West Virginia, and find ourselves sitting around the Sunday breakfast table with my sister and my father, tucking into fresh-baked biscuits, bacon, and scrambled eggs. I think of that quotation here, too, spending the weekend at Lost River, this gay-owned bed and breakfast in the hills of Hardy County, West Virginia.

An earthly heaven can be difficult to construct when your loves seem irreconcilable. For gays and lesbians in Appalachia who want to live full lives, who want to embrace both their gay and their mountain identities, who refuse to dismember themselves in order to assimilate, it can be very difficult to find some compromise between love of the same sex and love of home. If a gay man flees to the city, he is often encouraged to drop "that funny accent" and "those country ways," to feel ashamed of his mountain culture. If a lesbian stays in the mountains, she might face bigotry and abuse, especially from intolerant fundamentalist Christians; she might feel obliged to stay in the closet; she might suffer from the relative lack of social and romantic opportunities.

My compromise has been to live in university towns in Appalachia: Morgantown, West Virginia, for thirteen years, and now Blacksburg, Virginia, for the last fifteen. In such towns, I can feel safe in a liberal, intellectual atmosphere. As an academic, I can even combine my seemingly contradictory passions and teach both gay and lesbian literature and Appalachian studies. And I can stay in the mountains, close to what remains of my family, for, as Loyal Jones so eloquently points out in his famous essay "Appalachian Values," we hill folk are powerfully attached to our native places and our kin.

Lost River achieves a heaven that admits both a love for mountains and a love for men. In Hinton, as much as I cherish my family and the landscape of Summers County, I will never feel entirely welcome, entirely safe. It is a small town, full of folks who would more than object to the kind of man I am, and I have spent years arming myself with the emotional equivalent of a thistle's thorns against that kind of hatred. I have too many unpleasant high school memories to forgive that town: a split lip, a note pasted to my back stating "Kick Me, I'm Queer."

Here at Lost River, however, an entire gay enclave has grown up. It's one thing, after years of loneliness and romantic debacles, to finally find a lover and together to develop a protective circle of like-minded queer friends with whom to socialize. It's another thing entirely to find an active and open gay and lesbian community in Appalachia. Lost River is unique in this respect, at least in my experience. It is true that most of the members of this community are urban transplants—Lost River is only an hour or two from Washington, DC—but still I delight in being able to stay at a gay bed and breakfast or dine at a gay-owned restaurant without having to leave the mountains, without having to make the trip to Key West or Provincetown, New Orleans or Dupont Circle, Greenwich Village or the Castro. As much as I love those places, as often as I might want to escape to them for brief vacations, they are not Appalachia. I could never live there. They are not home.

❧

The pancakes and sausage are tasty, the gay camaraderie about the breakfast table boisterous and witty. This morning I'm wearing one of my Ajaxx 63 T-shirts, with "Butch County Forest Service" blazoned across my chest, a slogan many straight folks won't get. It combines those apparent antipodes, gay culture and rural life, and harkens back to my undergraduate days at West Virginia University, where I tried to satisfy contrary halves of my intellect by majoring in both English and forestry. Later, by the pool, I'll be reading *Rebel Yell 2*, a collection of short stories about gay men in the South. I am, in other words, immersing myself this Lost River weekend in All Things Queer, which is a delicious relief when one spends one's life entirely surrounded by straight, mainstream culture.

The sunny afternoon goes too quickly, as vacation time always does. Phil, Dan, John, and I vacillate among the hot tub, the chilly waters of the pool, Manhattans in plastic cups, and a few chapters in our magazines or books. For dinner, the four of us end up at the nearby Lost River Grill. Everything in the restaurant reflects the dual nature of this valley, the unusual combination of urban gay culture and native Appalachian ways. The owner is a handsome, well-built gay man who lives part of the week in Baltimore; the waitress is a local high school girl whose West Virginia accent and small-town friendliness immediately make me feel at home. The menu ranges from fairly exotic Mexican options to meat loaf, fried chicken, and other down-home specialties I grew up on, including—to my gourmand delight—a case full of homemade pies, including apple, peach, and coconut cream. The customers are either middle-aged and elderly Hardy County natives, usually heterosexual couples, or gay men and lesbians enjoying one another's company. Everyone seems to get along.

This peace was not instantly achieved, the owner tells us, as we gobble our tortillas and rib eyes. When he and his lover first bought the business, the local ministers encouraged their flocks to boycott the place. This unpleasant state of affairs lasted only a month, until the pious realized that the Lost River Grill was the only place in the valley to eat out. For once, the calorie-covetous flesh won out over the narrow-minded spirit. Appetite conquered prejudice.

Last summer at Lost River, I experienced prejudice of a different sort, reminding me of what an odd creature I am, cultural amphibian insisting on both worlds, Appalachian and queer. John and I were enjoying barbeque at another gay-owned establishment and chatting with a male couple from DC, when one of them said, "Well, you two can't be from West Virginia. You seem too literate." I smiled stiffly and raised my hand. "West Virginia here. I'm from Summers County. I teach Appalachian Studies at Virginia Tech." He had enough grace to be at least mildly embarrassed.

Alone with John later, I dropped my polite mask to snarl like any rural dweller, "Why the hell do these big-city folks come out here if they're just going to mock us? Why don't they just go home?" My resentment of such Appalachian stereotypes is only slightly less strong than my detestation for those country fundamentalists whose religious attitudes make life for many gays and lesbians miserable, full of loneliness, self-doubt, and fear.

Divided loyalties, perhaps. Still, I refuse to relinquish either world. I insist on it all. The late-summer pastures full of ironweed and goldenrod. Muscular, hairy, goateed men—just my type—marching in the West Virginia Gay Pride Parade. My father's gardens, the buckets of tomatoes and cucumbers he proudly brings home, the jars of spaghetti sauce and chowchow and corn relish he and my sister put up. Harness-strap boots, my black-leather motorcycle jacket, my leather-flag baseball cap. Listening to Tim McGraw, Brooks and Dunn, Melissa Etheridge, Joni Mitchell, Kathy Mattea as I drive my dusty pickup truck down winding West Virginia back roads. Harpers Ferry, Helvetia; San Francisco, Key West. Leather bars like Charleston's Tap Room or the Baltimore Eagle. "Poor Wayfaring Stranger," one of my few specialties on the lap dulcimer. Lobster and paté, brown beans and cornbread. *The*

Journal of Appalachian Studies, The Gay and Lesbian Review. In my life, at least, these contradictions coexist. They cannot be separated.

❧

For many, the desire might be to separate these poems, to set them apart, to tug out the references to mustaches and chest hair and stick to cornfields, ramps, and tomato stakes. As defiantly as I cling to both mountain and queer heritage, such segregation would be my first tendency, and, in the past, in the few volumes of poetry I've published, that has been my decision: "hillbilly" poems here, "queer" poems there. They seem incongruous, not to be mixed, like sodium and chlorine, chemicals that explode when combined.

Similarly, up to now I have published poetry *or* memoir, not a combination of the two. Indeed, some readers might prefer that I stick to one genre, not blend the two as I do in this book. Mixed-genre books are a rarity, an odd hybrid most agents and publishers would eye askance. No one knows quite what to do with them. Like gay Appalachians, such books resist simple labeling, simple pigeonholing.

Here, however, I have chosen to mix not only regional identity with sexual identity, but also poetry with prose, and these amalgams are a relief. It has been a difficult process, the work of decades, my attempts to make sense of the many complex and often contradictory facets of my personality. The hard-won integration resulting from that process is reflected not only in the content but in the form of this book. Mixed genre allows for many voices: the melancholy, romantic reflection, and solemnity of my poetry; the sharp humor, anger, political reflection, and storytelling of my prose; the necessary density of poetry; the roomier space of creative nonfiction. In order to more clearly meld the book's disparate elements, I have often borrowed phrases from related poems to title the segments of memoir, and hopefully the two genres here complement each other, memoir making more understandable the poems, poems lending greater depth to the memoir.

Thus, this collection is an attempt to reconcile my loves in my work as I have in my life. It is my attempt to construct the heaven that Carrie Bishop imagines, in which my passions—for the beauty of mountains and the beauty of men—may intertwine and, even in their tensions, achieve some kind of integrity, some tenuous wholeness. What I want is unity, however briefly achieved, like that cool morning at Lost River, drowsy horses standing in the mist, September dawn dripping from the trees, and the thistles, hardy as Highland warriors, enduring what they must, stoking their lavender fires, brandishing their swords, fusing in one stalk loveliness and ferocity.

Acknowledgments

"Sawing, the Last Day of Winter" was published in *Grab-a-Nickel.*

"Cornfield in March" and "Walking in Night Fog" were published in *Sulphur River Literary Review.*

"Creecy Greens" and "Mountain Fireflies" were published in *The Journal of Kentucky Studies.* "Mountain Fireflies" also appeared in *L'Attitude.* "Creecy Greens" also appeared in *Cooking Fresh from the Mid-Atlantic,* edited by Fran McManus and Wendy Rickard.

"Splitting Chestnut Oak," "Mizz Alice," and "Ambush" (previously titled "Tom's Creek Graveyard") were published in *Arts Alive! 2000: Anthology of New River Valley Writers and Poets,* edited by Elizabeth Spencer and Ann Goette.

"Bluestone Reservoir," "West Virginia Towns," "Chowchow" and "Turnip Greens" were published in *Pine Mountain Sand and Gravel.*

"The Cosmopolite and the Convict" and "Gathering Green Tomatoes in the Rain" were published in *Wind.*

"Allen," "Aeolian," "Sunday Sunlight" and "Duelling Feasts" were published in *BlackWater Review.*

"Helvetia" and "Ramps" were published in *Appalachian Journal.*

"Over Country-Fried Steak the Adulterer Retires," cowinner of the 1999 Food Verse Award, was published in *Literal Latté.*

"Weeds" was published in *Kestrel.*

"German Village" was published in *I Have My Own Song for It: Modern Poems of Ohio,* edited by Elton Glaser and William Greenway.

"Lemon Cake" and "Maple Syrup" were published in *Poetic Matrix.*

"Wild Magnolias" was published in *Crossing Troublesome: Twenty-five Years of the Appalachian Writers Workshop,* edited by Leatha Kendrick and George Ella Lyon.

"Goldenrod Seeds," second-place winner of the 2002 Appalachian Poetry Contest, was published in *Now and Then.*

"Bereft" was given an honorable mention in the 2002 Appalachian Poetry Contest sponsored by *Now and Then.*

"Bereft" and "Civilization Comes to Summers County" appeared in the *Spoon River Poetry Review.* "Dilly Beans" and "The Harvest of Motes" were published in *Appalachian Heritage.*

"Digging Potatoes" and "Summer Night" were published in *Confluence*.

"Tomato Stakes" was published in *Antietam Review*.

"Dilly Beans," "Digging Potatoes," and "Tomato Stakes" appeared in *Wild Sweet Notes: Fifty Years of West Virginia Poetry, 1950–1999*, edited by Barbara Smith and Kirk Judd.

"Homecoming" appeared in *Bloom*.

"Fried Chicken and Spoon Bread" appeared in *Walking Higher: Gay Men Write about the Deaths of Their Mothers*, edited by Alexander Renault.

"Hinton and Hejira," "Ephemera of Skin," "Loss and the Daily Biscuit," "Sunset over Hinton," "Her Kitchen's Square of Sunlight," "Redefining Home," and "The Silver in My Beard" appeared in *Small Town Gay: Essays on Family Life beyond the Big City*, edited by Elizabeth Newman.

"Emory and Henry" was published in *Rebel Yell 2: More Stories of Contemporary Southern Gay Men*, edited by Jay Quinn.

Several of these poems appeared in *Mountain Fireflies*, winner of the 1999 Poetic Matrix Chapbook Series.

Portions of this book appeared in "Haunted by Home," which was published in *Rebel Yell: Stories by Contemporary Southern Gay Authors*, edited by Jay Quinn, and in "Appalachian Subculture," which was published in the *Gay and Lesbian Review Worldwide*.

I owe a slew of folks:

My Virginia Tech colleagues—Lucinda Roy, Katherine Soniat, Lisa Norris, Gyorgyi Voros, Tiffany Trent, Simone Poirier-Bures, Ed Falco, Fred D'Aguiar, Robin Allnut, Aileen Murphy and Paul Heilker, Elizabeth Fine, Bernice Hausman, Shelli Fowler and Karen DePauw, Carl Bean, Steve and Jennifer Mooney, Grant Moss, Joseph Eska, Jim Collier and Monique Dufour, Alice Kinder, and Anita Puckett—for their delightful collegial company.

Virginia Tech staff Tammy Shepherd and Lynn Robinson, for their many kindnesses.

My former students Kim Murphy, Kellie Woodson, Heather Black, and Toby Quaranta, fighters all, for giving me hope.

Ennis McCrery, for Mill Mountain conversations and for good advice.

Ken Belcher and Darius Liptrap, Blacksburg Bear Buddies, for their mountaintop hospitality.

Zane Bagwell, Susie Bagwell, and Sarah Hasty Williams, for the Cambria Coven.

Winston Fuller and Louise Lamar-Fuller, Kevin Oderman and Sara Pritchard, Irene McKinney, Maggie Anderson, and Anna French, for their brilliance, their talent, and their encouragement.

Cathy Pleska, for gossip and camaraderie over cups of PollyPrissyPants tea.

Lynda Ann Ewen, Gillian Berchowitz, and David Sanders, for advice on the manuscript.

Phyllis Moore, Wild Yankee Woman, for her sweet tea and pepperoni rolls, and her tireless efforts to promote West Virginia writers.

John Peterson of Poetic Matrix Press, for publishing many of these poems in a chapbook, *Mountain Fireflies*.

Ann Smith, for loving her weird cousin no matter what.

Dan Connery, Phil Hainen, Donna Ross, and the Ross clan, for their friendship.

And, lastly, Joni Mitchell, Carly Simon, Melissa Etheridge, Tim McGraw, Steve Earle, Kathy Mattea, and Mary Chapin Carpenter, for the backroads music.

One

Summer Night

The last of spring clings in the child green
of the black willow, sagging into dark banks
over the New River, the sleep of blackbirds,
the white water's continuity.

In the depot light, railroad tracks gleam in and out,
dreaming of convergence, the nomad's insomnia.
By the baggage cart, an evening primrose winces open,
trickling aromas of fruit cereals and childhood,
mirages of destination.

Throughout the town, empty storefronts. Litter begins
to dervish. Headlights round a corner, a spider's web
ignites in the beam, electricity resolving the filament.

In our cubicles, the floor fan rattles all night.
Suffocating with moderation, we lean to the windows
to watch heat lightning whisper, to hear the C&O
drone after midnight, to gulp night air like some
black and cool liqueur poured from cut-glass decanters.

Even after our lids droop, we are waiting—
for the lightning's wink to resolve us,
for our bodies to flare into incandescence.

Hinton and Hejira

Mountain Lake, Virginia, summer 1998. I am teaching a course on Appalachian culture for Elderhostel students. A fine setting, this rustic stone resort high in the Alleghenies, and enthusiastic students, these retired folks much more eager to learn than many of my students at Virginia Tech. I discuss poetry by James Still and Maggie Anderson, fiction by Harriette Arnow and Lee Smith. Then I read a few of my own poems, the overtly Appalachian ones, the ones without gay references, the ones not likely to give offense. I can tell that they think I am a nice young man, and their image of me would be shattered, I fear, if they knew how fond I am of other nice young men.

For a break, in midafternoon I get out my dulcimer. As much as I want to spin out a fine yarn about how "this here dulcimer was carved by my granddaddy out of black walnut from the family farm, and he taught me all these songs when I was a child," today I confess to my audience that I am not some male Jean Ritchie, inheritor of a rich oral legacy. I discovered the dulcimer not through family or even regional tradition, but through the records of Joni Mitchell. This dulcimer, I gingerly admit, is a cheap mail-order version I bought long ago, when my undergraduate budget wouldn't allow me to buy the arts-and-crafts-fair home-built variety. The Elderhostelers are visibly disappointed.

After playing them a few folk ballads, I retune and play the dulcimer song I love the best, Joni's "A Case of You." The taste of Proust's madeleine was able to evoke memory, certainly, but, as has often been noted, so can a melody. Today I want to remember when I first heard the music of Joni Mitchell.

Not that day when this dulcimer was ordered from Elderly Instruments in Michigan, during my senior year in college. "Spruce top, mahogany back and sides," I used to chant to myself during the long walk from Lorenz Avenue to forestry classes at Percival Hall, dreaming of the day the instrument would arrive.

Not that evening in Cin's apartment when Will first showed me how to play "A Case of You." Will was a bearded, furry-chested friend of a friend whose sexuality was ambiguous enough to prevent me from making a pass, whose strong-armed hugs made me gasp and yearn for more.

Not those autumn evenings in the fall of 1977 in Sunnyside, Morgantown's student ghetto, when Allen, the first gay man who ever befriended me, played Joni's *Blue* again and again, and I fell in love with the album's lyrical sadness.

What I want is farther back. High school days, the time few gays and lesbians remember with fondness. My years at Hinton High School, in the mid-1970s.

❦

It must have been the fall of 1976, as far as I can gauge from this distance. Where did I find it, *Hejira*, the first Joni Mitchell album I ever bought? A local drugstore, I suspect. Up till then, I'd listened to the Carpenters, the Partridge Family, Elton John, Neil Diamond. But, to use the southern phrase, I was, that autumn, "standin' in need" of more intelligent, more complex, more literate music to keep me company, to soften my loneliness and melancholy, to shore up my dreams of escape. "Hejira" means, after all, a journey undertaken to flee hostility or danger. I stumbled onto Joni's haunting collection of travel-themed songs at a time when good books and moving music were almost all I had, when my emotional isolation felt almost complete, when travel to somewhere more welcoming constantly composed my daydreams.

What made this loneliness more piercing was that it followed months of queer camaraderie, the sweet siblinghood of misfits, a hard thing to find in southern West Virginia in any decade. I had had a circle of supportive lesbian friends, but that circle was by then for the most part dispersed. Jo had been forced to leave her teaching position at Hinton High by the homophobic principal, a man I detest to this day. Bill and Kaye, a class ahead of me, had graduated and moved on to attend West Virginia University (WVU), sending me letters about their discovery of a gay bar and the new queer friends they were making. I lived for those letters. They made me sick with envy, but they gave me hope. One day, I knew, it would be my turn to "get my gorgeous wings and fly away," as Joni put it. But I was stuck in Hinton, West Virginia, to complete my senior year before I could flee to WVU myself.

Only Laurie remained, a younger lesbian who lived nearby. Every evening we met in the park and walked across a bridge recently built over the New River. No matter how cold the night, we sat on the concrete railing, watched the black water rush by below, discussed the unfortunately straight boys and girls we found attractive, and wondered how our distant friends were doing in the brave new world of university life. Surely somewhere in Morgantown, I thought, I would meet an attractive man worth loving, a man who would meet my hot urge to touch with an eager urge of his own.

❦

Hinton is an isolated railroad town along the New River. Then and now, about thirty-five hundred people live there, most of them conservative and religious, most of them, I would imagine, hostile to gays. It is like many small towns in and out of Appalachia: it is dangerous to be openly queer there. To this day, as big and mean, bearded, booted, and leather clad as I have become (look tough and people are more likely to leave you alone), I feel ill at ease, paranoid when I am in Hinton, especially now that I have published a good bit of openly gay material, especially now that my editorial-writing father has referred to my sexuality in his newspaper essays attacking fundamentalism and homophobia. As much as I muse on the warrior archetype, delight vicariously in handsome Aragorn's swordplay in the *Lord of the Rings* films, and relish the revenge fantasies allowed by writing and reading fiction, I realize that in reality I am outnumbered.

I was neither big nor mean when I met Jo Davison, the teacher who was to become my lesbian mentor. I was a shy, quiet, plump, insecure, unattractive, bookish kid, with long, dark, rebellious hair, good southern manners, and no sense at all of the warrior mentality that a hostile world would someday inspire in me. Davison, who'd been teaching biology at Hinton High for several years, had founded an ecology club in which my older cousin Ann participated, and one day Ann, having decided most probably that I spent too much time studying, invited me along on a club jaunt.

It was, I think, on a Saturday morning in the spring of 1975 that Jo and I officially met. Her blue Gremlin pulled up to the Forest Hill post office, where I waited at the preappointed time, Ann gestured me inside, and off the three of us went, armed with a detailed road map, to track down abandoned cars for A. James Manchin's REAP program. All day we bumped down rough back roads, knocked on doors, got permission forms signed, and spray painted a green theta, the ecology club symbol, on those old wrecks the owners had agreed to let the state dispose of.

Jo must have liked something about me, or recognized my queer potential, so to speak, because soon I was encouraged to become a regular member of the ecology club. During my sophomore year, I spent just about every Saturday working on nature trails, learning to identify trees, picking up roadside litter, or enjoying hot dog roasts with other club members. Eventually, I became one of an inner circle of students who hung around Jo's home on some Sundays, a home she shared with another woman, Robbi. Robbi was, supposedly, Jo's ward.

And eventually Jo came out to me. Inspired by a textbook controversy in Kanawha County, West Virginia, in which local fundamentalists had tried to control what textbooks might be used in public schools, she had begun writing the *Colony* trilogy, a series of novels set in a future controlled by Christian fundamentalists, long hunt-and-peck typewritten manuscripts that she let me read. In her fiction, freethinkers escape this theocratic society and create their own hidden community, a colony in the Canadian Rockies. At one point in the second novel, two of the female characters, to my surprise at the time, become lovers. In the third novel, almost all the main characters are lesbians. Jo was taking a great risk showing such material to a high school student in a small rural town—show such subversive texts to the wrong student, the easily shocked student with the big mouth and the devout parents, and you're liable to be run out of town. But she had judged her audience well. Raised by liberal parents on nonconformist treatises by nineteenth-century American transcendentalists, I responded only with curiosity and a desire for more information. I even asked if she had any books about male homosexuals. It was then that Jo lent me Patricia Nell Warren's novel *The Front Runner.*

❧

In May 2003 I attended the first Saints and Sinners Literary Festival in New Orleans, an event featuring gay and lesbian writers. At the opening reception a friend introduced me to Patricia Nell Warren, and I was momentarily speechless. How could I tell this woman, without a fan's awkward spluttering, how much her work had changed my life? I did my best—not my most articulate moment—and Warren kindly posed with me for a photo when my partner, seizing the opportunity, whipped out his digital camera.

The Front Runner, published in 1974, was one of the first novels to deal intelligently, compassionately, and realistically with a male homosexual relationship. The narrator, Harlan Brown, describes his attraction to his star runner, Billy Sive, who's training for the Olympics; their eventual relationship; and the scandal it causes. Jo, in lending me that novel, saved me years of self-doubt, self-loathing, fear, and confusion. I read that dog-eared paperback in only a few days, and, when I finished, I'd fallen in love with Billy Sive, and I had begun to understand yearnings that I had always dismissed before as admiration or envy. I found a name for what some men made me feel. Unnamed, an emotion can stay inchoate, nebulous; it can sink back into oblivion. Named, a passion takes on force, meaning, depth, and direction.

What a life-saving gift, the gift of self-knowledge. Sometimes it destroys, as it did Oedipus. In my case, it gave me first the rich camaraderie of exiles, those times spent with Jo and my fellow misfits of the Colony (as we called both our circle of friends and Davison's farmhouse). When those friends left town and the Colony dispersed, self-knowledge gave me bitter isolation and deepened my desperate yearning for a place and time far from Hinton, that scenic but intolerant mountain town. I learned the survival techniques of gay high schoolers: lies, omissions, subterfuge, protective coloration, a skilled peripheral vision with which to admire men on the sly. I read gay-themed novels to escape the all-encompassing straight world: Patricia Nell Warren's *The Fancy*

Dancer, about a sexy, black-leather-clad hero who seduces a priest; Mary Renault's *The Persian Boy,* told from the point of view of Alexander the Great's young lover. I lay on my bed in the dark—traditional position of the alienated adolescent—listened to Joni sing "Refuge of the Roads," and dreamed of a day when my escape would be more than mental.

I escaped Hinton. I fled to Morgantown and West Virginia University, where I stayed for undergraduate and graduate schools. I found no magically welcoming gay paradise, no passionately reciprocal relationship such as that shared by Billy Sive and Harlan Brown. Only brief flings, shared lust, three or four unrequited loves, the smoke of seedy gay bars. Setting my hopes on the larger arena of the big city, I briefly escaped Appalachia. I taught at George Washington University during the fall semester of 1985, was dismayed by the coldness of the faculty, the mercenary obsessions of city dwellers, the constant irritants of urban life. At the beginning of the Christmas holidays, I rode Amtrak back through the slate-gray hills and heaved my luggage down off the train and onto the station platform at Hinton. The gay world had disappointed me, so I returned to the only place I knew. Somehow I would have to make my peace with home. If men could not love me, then I would learn to live without love. I would devote myself to the beauty of landscape.

"I could drink a case of you," goes Joni's song. I cannot sing it—the melody is far too complex for my untrained voice—but the Elderhostelers seem to enjoy the strummed dulcimer chords. The afternoon session is almost ended. Soon, time to walk around the lake. John will be done with classes soon and will drive up here to Mountain Lake for cocktails, dinner, and a night with me in the rough-stone lodge. What will the Elderhostelers make of him? I wonder. I am dark and he is light. We could not be mistaken for brothers.

Emory and Henry

It was the year America turned two hundred, the summer of freedom celebrations and especially grand Fourth of July parties. When I think of 1976, however, what I remember is not so much bicentennial excitement as a small college in southwest Virginia and my first vivid taste of homophobia. Even in America, I was to discover, living freely and honestly has its risks. Even in America, I realized, I do not wholly belong.

That spring—it was my junior year at Hinton High School—Jo Davison had lent me that momentous novel *The Front Runner*, and I'd realized that I was gay. College was still over a year away, but meanwhile there was a briefer escape in the offing. Davison was a biology teacher, an excellent one, in whose class I'd excelled, and she encouraged me to apply for a National Science Foundation (NSF) biology honors program at Emory and Henry College.

I was accepted, to my delight. In early June of 1976 my parents drove me the few hours through dramatically mountainous countryside to the college, dropped me off at the boys' dorm, Armbrister House, and soon departed. I sat in the porch swing and watched them drive off, both excited and a little frightened to be on my own for the first time, far from family, friends, and home. That evening, after orienting myself with a campus stroll, I met my roommates—Jim, from New York, and Kenny, from Narrows, Virginia—then began to unpack.

At an introductory meeting the next morning, all the students met Dr. Jones, a biology teacher at Emory and Henry, who had organized the NSF program and who would teach most of the classes. It would last for six weeks, and twenty students would participate. Along with daily classes in botany, microbiology, forestry, and other branches of the life sciences, Dr. Jones had scheduled trips to many local spots of cultural and biological interest: Abram's Falls, Mount Rogers, Saltville's strip mines, Abingdon's Barter Theater, and Lake Norris, Tennessee, where we would have a week's worth of study.

There was just enough spare time for me to feel headily independent. I rose early some mornings to jog around the misty track, thinking of my *Front Runner* hero Billy Sive. I wandered around the picturesque campus, admiring its huge old trees, its stream, its columned brick buildings. One evening I attended an organ recital in the campus chapel, sitting alone in the balcony, where early mornings and late nights of study caught up with me and I fell asleep on the pew. After meals in the cafeteria, I'd head down to the pond to visit Luther, an ill-tempered white swan, who would dutifully bite my boot when I thrust my foot within range of his vicious beak. One evening, straddling a wall near the pond, feeling a little homesick, I looked down to discover, scratched in the stone, the name of an ecology club friend of mine from back home, a girl who'd attended the very same program two summers before. The serendipity was comforting.

Having spent my entire life in Appalachia, I found it very stimulating to meet students from other areas of the country. All five kids from New York were Jewish, and this I found especially interesting. For me, Jews were an exotic breed, since I'd rarely encountered them in small-town West Virginia, and the same intellectual curiosity I applied to my class work drove me to ask many questions about their culture and religion. One girl in particular I grew fond of, Sue, from Syosset, on Long Island. She had long black hair and a big smile. Around her neck she wore a *chi*, a Hebrew letter whose significance she was to explain, along with many other details of Jewish history.

Sue and I were quite simpatico. What a luxury it was to spend time with someone so intelligent. One evening we inadvertently caused a thrill of gossip to run through the group. After a long talk in the lounge of the girls' dorm, we stretched out at opposite ends of a couch, covered by the same blanket, listening to Chicago's "Color My World" in candlelight. Drowsing, we heard a door creak. An eavesdropper, apparently, for soon the word was that Sue and I were dating.

It was no wonder that Sue and I were suspected of a romantic or erotic entanglement, for, within the first few weeks of the NSF program, with the tide of flirtation waxing high, several of the boys and girls in the group of twenty had coupled off. We were living in a hothouse environment, certainly. Pumped full of the hormones of late adolescence to begin with, we were living together, eating together, studying together, going to classes together, traveling together: circumstances conducive to dangerously intense feelings.

I wasn't interested in using Sue as a cover for my homosexuality, however. Instead, fairly early in the six-week program, I'd come out both to her and to Lisa, a pretty, big-breasted girl from Aliquippa, Pennsylvania, whom I was to nickname "Sweetums" for her perpetually sunny personality. The other girls, unaware of my queer inclinations, must have regarded me as possible dating material. I assume this only because Sue reported one day that the girls had all methodically rated the guys and had come to the conclusion that, since I had the hairiest legs, I must also have the biggest "bird." I had just enough adolescent macho pride to be pleased at this report, though I wasn't interested in presenting my bird to any of my female classmates.

In fact, I wasn't all that interested in my male classmates, or very many other boys my age. Instead, my lust focused on older men, on several of the college students who were attending summer school at Emory and Henry. Some evenings after studying, I'd head down to the tennis courts and sit in the bleachers to watch sweaty young men bound about in the humid twilight. At some point in the failing light, lamps would switch on, about which the summer moths would crazily congregate. Occasionally, a few of the athletes would strip to the waist, and I, feigning interest in the game, would move a little closer to study the fur on their chests and bellies, the stubble on their cheeks, the way the muscles in their backs and shoulders moved. Instead of taking such beautiful flesh into my mouth, I was consigned by age and shyness to fantasy, to metaphor: the hard curves of their biceps were river-smoothed stones, their moist body hair was dark orchard grass, mosses, fern fronds, the spring-soft needles of larch. I had never touched a man before, not in the way I wanted to, and sitting there in the dark, stiff beneath my denim shorts, I would try to imagine how they tasted, how they smelled. I had no idea how to approach them, what to say that might encourage their interest, their consent.

One college student in particular grabbed my interest that summer. He much resembled the way I envisioned Billy Sive from *The Front Runner:* tanned, lithe, with a head of golden-brown curls and long, fine-muscled legs glistening with golden hair. Several of the girls in our NSF group clustered about him when they could, usually after lunch in the cafeteria, and I envied them their femaleness, only because it licensed them to flirt with desirable men. I had grown up around enough intolerant straight men to guess how he was likely to receive my lusty admiration, so I kept it to myself.

He was strikingly handsome and he knew it, showing off his body as often as possible in skimpy tank tops and tiny running shorts. One especially hot afternoon, when I strolled down to the duck pond to offer my boot to the savage swan's snapping beak, my idol was lounging in the shade beneath an oak with another coterie of undergrad girls. He had nothing on but blue nylon swim trunks. At sixteen, out barely four months, I was already a chest man. I walked past with exaggerated slowness, thankful for the way that sunglasses conceal a randy stare, and devoured him with the only sense I could. His nipples were glossy and nut brown, his tanned torso hairless except for the trail to happiness, as I had already learned to call it, the ridge of golden fur that bisected his lean belly and disappeared into the top of his nicely packed shorts.

The next time I saw him, several days later, was in the cafeteria, sitting a few tables down with more admirers. In the first of what has proven to be twenty-five years' worth of wicked techniques for spying on men's bodies, I deliberately dropped my fork on the floor, then bent beneath the table to fetch it. There they were, a few yards away, those long, delicious runner's legs. For a minute I thought of dropping to the floor myself, crawling through the forest of calves, and running my tongue up his thigh before tugging his revealing shorts down with my teeth. Needless to say, I thought better of it. Still, as I returned to my lunch, I regretted living in a world in which such libidinous acts occur not at all often, a world in which I would not discover how such a man might feel as he stripped us both and then lay on top of me naked.

While I wrestled with my hormones, occasionally finding some solitary relief in the shower, I was also experiencing many novelties, the presence of which makes most youthful years seem effervescent and many adulthoods fall a bit flat. Along with classes in genetics and ecology, we enjoyed regular jaunts off campus. In Saltville, Virginia, we drove about a strip-mined site and learned about the deleterious environmental effects of coal mining. We climbed Mount Rogers, the highest mountain in Virginia, and in the process I discovered how gullible city kids are. They were ridiculously afraid of a herd of cows we passed in a field on our way to the top, and when they pointed to cow pies and asked what they were, I took the opportunity to explain that the French use such soft and fragrant fungi in sauces and salads. I recommended that they do the same upon their return home, though where in downtown Manhattan they might find such ripe produce I did not know.

One day in class Dr. Jones passed out tickets, and later that afternoon he and his assistants drove us to Abingdon, Virginia, for a play at the Barter Theater, so called because during the Depression, when it was founded, the poor would pay for tickets with homegrown vegetables. After a tour of the quaint town and a glimpse of the elegant Martha Washington Inn, we settled into our seats in the theater. The performance that evening was a series of dramatic readings from *Transformations*, Anne Sexton's sardonic take on the Brothers Grimm, accompanied by Walter Carlos's *Sonic Seasonings*. My first taste of both modern poetry and electronic music. I was entranced. The world was beginning to widen. And I knew, even more vividly than before, that the small town where I had grown up could never satisfy me, could never give my mind or my body what they craved.

Another afternoon in late June we all hiked to Abram's Falls. After a walk along a path through thick woods, a good opportunity to learn some of the native plant species, we came to an overlook. Below, across a shady dell, creek water poured dramatically over a rocky lip, smashing into foam on rocks below. Several hippie hikers who'd gotten there before us had climbed onto a ledge behind the waterfall's translucent veil. One of them, in the dim emerald light, stripped off his soaked T-shirt, pulled off his boots, and, clad now only in faded denim shorts, stepped forward into the cascade. Laughing and gasping, he backed out of the pounding water, then stepped in again, his long brown hair plastered to his shoulders, the creek running its clear fingers down his chest and back. He was the image of a forest god, a satyr, and I wanted to join him in his freedom and his ecstasy. A shaggy kid with straggling teenaged beard and thick glasses, I wanted to strip and enter the waterfall, become someone else, someone equally desirable, make love to him on carpets of moss.

A week later, the big day came, America's birthday, and we all were invited over to Dr. Jones's house for a cookout. One of the girls, Charlotte, arrived wearing a T-shirt that brazenly announced, "Fuck the Bicentennial." I found this disconcerting, for my mother had long forbade me to use that word in public, much less let it grace an article of clothing. But, inspired by this naughty example, several of us, over hot dogs and pop, shared lyrics to vulgar songs when Dr. Jones's back was turned: "Gonna tell you all a story 'bout a man named Jed. He raped Ellie May and he threw her on the bed." Afterward, a few of us, on a dare, wandered tentatively through a nearby cemetery in the misty, firefly-haunted dark. When I returned to my dorm room alone, I stretched out on the bed and listened to the radio. The Carpenters sang "I Know I Need to Be in Love." Pulling off my shirt in the summer heat, I stood in the dark before the mirror, running my fingers over a chest still a stranger to hair or gym workouts, wondering when and how I would lose my hated virginity.

I was to discover, like most queer youth, the pains of being gay long before the pleasures, however. Having realized the nature of my sexuality only months before, I took to Emory and Henry's library in the first weeks of the NSF program to track down information on homosexuality. Emboldened by ignorance, youthful optimism, and a blithe disregard for the world's disapproval, I didn't go to any great efforts to conceal my reading material. Surely I would be safe from prejudice on the campus of such a bastion of learning.

One evening as I returned from such a library raid, I ran into Tonia, a tall, pretty classmate with long red hair, a spoiled air, and a sharp sense of humor. "What are you reading?" she asked, eyeing my armful of books. I showed her. She wrinkled her nose, then headed off with a piece of news destined to dwarf any other gossip our group had eagerly tossed about that summer.

It took less than twenty-four hours. After a class on microbes the next afternoon, our group dispersed. Most headed out to relax before dinner, but a few lingered in the hall of the biology building. I was talking to Lisa about the next assignment when another classmate, Steve, wandered up. I hadn't gotten to know him very well, but I had noticed, during an afternoon of water volleyball in the campus pool, that he had a fine body, pale, smooth and lightly muscled; that he thus looked almost as appealing as an adult in his form-fitting swimsuit; and that he was a skilled, almost poetic, diver.

"So, Jeff, I hear you're having a gay old time at the library this summer," Steve said snidely. "What's it like to like boys?"

I flushed with shock and stood speechless. Lisa, however, was far from paralyzed. Rustling up some of the odd insults of her Pennsylvanian hometown, she spat, "That's none of your business, is it? And how'd you like to kiss my ass, you hoopie, you numnard, you heeneyhocker!" Steve instantly retreated before this linguistic barrage, this indignant buxom amazon. He turned tail, scuttling down the stairwell and out the door. It was not the first time, nor the last, that men would cause me pain and women would take my part.

I was too young to know what to expect. Had I known, I might have hidden my library books more carefully, despite all my high-flown nonconformist principles. What I got was not violence, or even the threat of violence—we were all too scholarly and well brought up for that—but avoidance, whispers, averted eyes. Never again anything as crudely blunt as Steve's comment. Rather, all the body language that makes one aware of one's status as a pariah.

In the difficult days that followed, Sue and Lisa stood by me, of course, very deliberately sitting with me in the cafeteria and in classes. Katie, from Knoxville, a girl with big glasses and bobbed hair, and Lauren, from Silver Spring, a good-looking athletic girl with long Scandinavian braids, also seemed supportive. Of all the boys, only Travis seemed not to care about the rumors. An awkward, skinny, bookish boy with a big Adam's apple and nerd glasses, he'd grown up in the tiny community of Meadows of Dan, Virginia, where he'd probably endured enough ribbing to make him sympathetic to any outcast's plight.

My greatest nemesis was Ira, an unattractive kid from New York with an annoying accent and a sense of entitlement. He never said anything to me directly, probably because I had a bigger build than he did. However, my female friends reported that, in my absence, he was the most insulting of the crew, a baby homophobe. I thought of infant copperheads, whose venom is virulent and ready for the using as soon as they hatch. I hated Ira. I wanted to break his arms and feed him to Luther, who would hold him under the pond's scummy waters with his beautiful white wings till the bubbling stopped and the pond's surface was smooth again.

My roommates Jim and Kenny were the greatest martyrs in the midst of this mess, for they had to share their room with an apparent monster. They began dressing, both morning and evening, in the bathroom down the hall, rather than allowing me glimpses of their skinny, hollow-chested, adolescent bodies—glimpses that, they must have imagined, would madden me as a matador might a bull. With no other place to sleep, they must have lain in bed staring at the ceiling, only yards from the dozing dragon. Did they think that I might descend on them as soon as they'd drifted off, to suck their blood, their breath?

This unpleasant situation built to a head pretty quickly. One evening, as I was stretched out on my bed reading, Travis came by and whispered that there was a meeting about to begin downstairs, a meeting Ira had called, a meeting to which I had not been invited. When Travis hurried out, I lay back, stared at the maple leaves filling the windows, and listened to dorm-room doors slam and footsteps descend the stairs. Travis, Ira, Jim, Kenny, Steve, Jeremy.

A long time passed. I gave up any pretense of reading. Though I didn't really expect violence, it did occur to me that I had never struck anyone before in my life, that it was a long drop from my windowsill to the ground. I was too young, too ignorant of history, to realize how ironic it was that Ira, a Jew, was spearheading this persecution. He would have popped me into a concentration camp in a heartbeat.

Then footsteps ascended the stairs. One set of footsteps, surely a good sign. Would whoever it was be brandishing a torch, a crucifix, or, in Ira's case, a Star of David? If only I had a vampire's fangs. At this point, I'd use them not to drain vital juices but, like any cornered beast, to rend.

It was Dr. Jones's assistant, Chris, who served as the boys' RA. On his shoulders had fallen this uncomfortable duty. The NSF program and its intense togetherness would be continuing for another three weeks. He couldn't dismiss me, because I'd done nothing but check out library books, like any good student. Somehow he had to make peace.

He did so by ignoring the truth and encouraging everyone in the program to do the same. Denial. It does save lives. The boys were concerned, they'd come to him, he gently explained. "But I can't believe that you're a homosexual choosing to make your presence known," Chris stated flatly. Perhaps he thought I would have to be effeminate, crinoline clad, to be truly queer. Perhaps only a rigorous routine of mincing and tittering would convince him. Or perhaps he realized that I was indeed gay and that the best thing to do under the circumstances was to encourage me to officially renounce an identity that had proven dangerous. I felt like Galileo: Yes, the earth is flat. Chris was asking me to lie to make life easier for all of us.

I wouldn't lie and claim to be straight, but I wouldn't insist on my homosexuality either. He'd given us both an out, an early version of "Don't ask, don't tell." I was sixteen years old, I was frightened, I was not a career activist, I was far away from supportive queer friends. So I said nothing. I gave him the silence he needed to smooth things over.

Chris left briefly, only to herd up my two roommates Jim and Kenny. "Now, shake hands and let's forget this misunderstanding," Chris insisted. As Jim stepped forward and gingerly gripped my hand, our eyes met. His face was flushed, his stare was full of fear. I couldn't believe it. He was terrified of me. I, who was not yet bitter, angry, and irritable, as I am at forty-five. Still the sixteen-year-old Jeff, I was a nonviolent idealist, a shy intellectual, a southern boy who tried to be polite and kind in every situation. It would take me many years to realize that such fear, in different degrees and different circumstances, is the sort that sometimes kills.

Everyone seemed grateful to escape this unpleasantness, and, in the remaining weeks of the program, the topic surfaced only rarely. Tonia, the gossip queen whose loose tongue had started the semiscandal, attempted suicide for no reason the rest of us were ever to learn, and within days she was sent home.

We remaining students spent a week at a biology field station near Norris Lake, Tennessee, studying limnology with a local expert who discoursed on lake microorganisms and aquatic plants. One day, to my amazement, I discovered a dead scorpion on the floor of the lab. Recalling my father's stories of his World War II days in the Sahara and such creatures' penchant for dark sleeping places, I idly wondered if I could coax one into Ira's shoe the next time he took a nap. Then, as now, I have a crippling inability to forgive.

One morning, Sally, a quiet classmate, did a sudden cartwheel as she, Sue, and I strolled through a clearing toward the classroom. Her shirt briefly slipped up, exposing bare breasts. How much simpler life must be, I mused, for those boys who would find that sight arousing. That afternoon, as we all floated about the lake in a pontoon boat, a sudden thunderstorm broke loose. I sat on the deck in my swimsuit, cross-legged, head thrown back, welcoming the passionate violence of the sky, surges of rain crashing over me like the foamy cascades of Abram's Falls. Laughing and shivering, I knew what I felt was ecstasy, a taste of things to come.

On the drive back to the field station, a crescent moon rose with silver certainty over a tobacco barn's silhouette. One more night there, time to enjoy a bonfire, songs, marshmallows, to listen to crickets and watch fireflies flicker. Then back to the campus of Emory and Henry for a few more days of class. Our time together was almost up.

The afternoon we returned from Norris Lake, I sat on the porch swing reading Hermann Hesse's novel *Demien*. Kenny joined me on the swing with a book of his own. A few minutes passed in studious silence. Then, stretching, I rested my arm across the back of the swing. Kenny looked around nervously. Did he think that, blind with desire, I was trying surreptitiously to work my arm around him in order to slip my hand down his shirt? "Oh, for God's sake!" I snarled. "Sorry," he blushed, moving to the opposite end of the swing, and then, by slow degrees, with studied casualness, onto the porch steps and so out into the shade of the nearest tree. No use taking a chance when the possibility of infection might be present.

The last evening of the NSF program, in an old cabin on the campus, we shared a farewell dinner, during which tongue-in-cheek awards were given out. I received "The Gayest," which Ira announced before passing over the mock certificate. Everyone laughed nervously. I smiled good-naturedly, thinking of Luther, the truly vicious killer swan, the churning pond waters, the shrieks subsiding to silence. I would never have to see these kids again.

But a few I would heartily miss, after six intense weeks together. At the dinner's end, Knoxville Katie hugged me hard and whispered, "You're cool, don't you forget it," before heading off to pack. The next morning Sue and Lisa left early, and I saw them off. As she stepped into her mother's car, Sue took off her *chi* necklace and put it around my neck. I watched the cars disappear, then sat alone on the steps of the biology building in the thick fog of a summer dawn and cried.

❦

For several years I corresponded with my Emory and Henry favorites, before our lives sped up in college and we eventually lost touch. In one letter Katie confessed to me that she had recently realized that she was bisexual and thanked me for enduring what I had that summer, for it had helped her come to terms with her own sexuality. Sue told me of a minireunion in New York in 1978, a car ride during which Ira had discussed me contemptuously and a drunken Lauren, from the back seat, had growled, "So what's so wrong with homosexuality?" thus effectively shutting him up. I like to think that flaxen-haired amazon has delighted many a lesbian since I last saw her, and Ira, though lucky enough to have escaped Luther's voracity, has long ago fallen prey to a snapping piranha swarm of predatory drag queens.

In March of 1999 I attended the Appalachian Studies Association Conference in Abingdon, Virginia, the first time I'd been back to that part of the state since 1976. When I presented my paper on gay life in Appalachia, I was applauded strenuously by an audience composed of many gays and lesbians. Their enthusiasm was, I suspect, less a comment on the paper's quality than it was evidence that there are many mountain queers who are desperately eager to read material on a topic so little acknowledged or discussed. Afterward, my lover John and I spent the night at the luxurious Martha Washington Inn, last seen when I was sixteen. That evening we attended a performance at the Barter Theater, and I thought of that teenager hearing for the first time the work of Anne Sexton, a writer who would teach him how effectively a poet can use pain.

On the way home, John and I drove through the campus of Emory and Henry. The layout of the buildings came back to me in a rush: the boys' dorm, the biology building, the library brimful of dangerous books, the chapel, cafeteria, and duck pond. No sign of Luther in the gray wintry drizzle, no bare-chested boys lunging about on the tennis courts, no *Front Runner* look-alike. He's probably plump, balding, and married like myself. Perhaps his son is now as old as he was the day I saw him shirtless, lounging in the hot shade beneath the oak trees.

This November, at a friend's invitation, I will be reading poetry at Emory and Henry, almost twenty-five years after my memorable summer there. I will wear Sue's *chi* beneath a suitably academic dress shirt and blazer. When I look over the audience, I will remember their faces, the ones who knew me for six weeks in 1976, when I was still a sheltered boy, the ones who treated me with kindness. I will try to imagine, in one empty seat (for there are always those at poetry readings), that boy himself, shaggy, sparsely bearded, frightened into silence. When he looks up at me and smiles, I will begin to speak.

Appalachian Beard Stubble

The poems have always shifted back and forth between the beauty of nature and the beauty of men. First was a scrawled poem titled "Crocuses under Concrete." It was composed in a bored moment in seventh-grade study hall and was inspired by my father, who had recently complained about all the asphalt and concrete of urban America. "Imagine the millions of seed sprouts and flower bulbs growing toward the surface only to encounter a barrier of concrete," he'd mused. Built to grow toward light, but trapped in darkness. Fit metaphor for any number of lives.

Later in high school, the love poems began. I yearned after a dark-haired boy in my Latin class, one of those black-eyed, swarthy charmers all the girls swooned over. How I prized the brief sentence he wrote in my senior yearbook. The poems I wrote about him were the only way I had to touch him and the only way I could express what I felt.

Phys ed, otherwise a torture for an uncoordinated scholar like me, became a prime source of erotic excitement. I ran my starved eyes like eager hands along the bodies of other boys in the showers. I relished shirts and skins in basketball, watching the muscles in Billy's chest shift as he bounded down the court for a fine layup. One afternoon we played tag football on the lawn by Hinton's war memorial. I still remember the diamond-shaped patch of sweaty dark hair between Alan's pecs when he stripped to the waist amidst a swarm of migrating monarch butterflies that suddenly encompassed us on their way south.

Another inspiration for both poetry and futile sexual fantasy was my buddy Mike, an active member of the ecology club Jo Davison had formed. Mike wasn't really an outcast like the rest of Jo's favorite students; he was a handsome, popular football player, with a string of girlfriends. But some sense of right, combined with an innate streak of wildness, must have convinced him to become our protector. I was a quiet A student, and most of my other friends were discernibly lesbian, so we were constantly threatened and mocked. Mike stood up for us. When his football-team buddies insulted us, he brightly told them to kiss his lily-white ass. Most of us had not chosen our outcast status. He, on the other hand, had deliberately bucked convention and taken a stand, show-ing a rebellious courage I always admired.

I also, quietly and passionately, admired his looks. Mike was the apotheosis of all that is best and most appealing in mountain men. He had dark hair, a catfish grin, constant beard stubble in warm weather, and, in winter, a fine thick beard. In town, he strode around in ratty jeans, boots, and denim jackets. Occasionally, at Davison's farm, where the Colony hung out, he worked on his perpetually ailing old car. Invariably, he stripped to the waist, revealing big muscles and dark hair spreading lyrically over his chest and belly. When he crawled out from under the automobile innards, his shoulder or cheek would be streaked with oil. Yet, belying this deliciously rough exterior, he was bright, brave, and kind. An irresistible ideal, that combination of scruffy toughness and compas-sionate heart.

Mike was both a role model for me and an early infatuation. One winter day I hunted deer with him on the mountain above the Colony farmhouse. A baby butch, my lesbian friends would have called me, as I proudly sported my new Case XX knife, and though I prayed we would find no deer, I was very pleased that he'd invited me along. Spring of 1976, at a school camping trip to North Bend State Park, this mentor by the campfire ritualized our relationship by solemnly presenting me with my first bottle of alcohol. Annie Green Springs Berry Frost, I be-lieve it was, appropriate syrup for a beginning drinker. I gulped it down my throat as if it were his masculinity I was consuming. That summer, around another campfire, in the midnight heat he pulled off his shirt, and as I sipped whiskey with him, I watched the firelight and the shadow play across his muscles and thought about Plato, how beauty reveals God.

In high school, I was never brave enough to make a pass, but once I went to college and became a swaggering leather-stud-in-training, I planned to get Mike drunk on Canadian Lord Calvert, his favorite whis-key, and seduce him when we both returned to Hinton over Christmas break. He never showed up, and, true anticlimax, I haven't seen him since high school. I gather from town talk that he's been married and divorced, has traveled a lot, rarely comes back to town. Nevertheless, over twenty years later, I'm grateful for the inspiration and the instruction. An early icon in my sexual and aesthetic development, he helped compose that constellation of elements that, for me, define the desirable.

Beginner's Wine

It was hard to come back to Hinton after I'd graduated from high school and had had a taste of gay community in Morgantown. I loved hanging out with Bill and Cin, Laura and Allen at the Fox, sipping tequila sunrises and other high-sugar, low-alcohol novice drinks, dreaming about some handsome man across the room I was far too shy to approach. I thought of Hinton with loathing. It was a place where I would have to lie to stay alive. In fact, eager to distance myself from Summers County and to immerse myself in queerdom, I spent Thanksgiving break of my freshman year with lesbian friends in Gauley Bridge, inspiring my favorite cousin, Ann, to write me a sharp-tongued letter about how I'd broken my grandmother's heart, a letter I still think of with wincing shame. There are disadvantages to being part of a close-knit family.

Without employment in Morgantown, I spent the summer after my freshman year in my hometown. My gay identity and queer aesthetic had become solid constructs by that point. I was not some confused kid in the process of coming out. I knew what I wanted. And so, suddenly, the male beauty I craved was everywhere. Those country boys I lusted after rarely dispensed with their customary boots and jeans, even in hot weather, but they needed little excuse to peel off their shirts. This only deepened my obsession with bare chests. Shirtless men hoeing in their cornfields, shirtless men fishing hip deep in the New River's jade currents, shirtless men driving dustily by in their pickup trucks. Studying the dark swirls of fur matting their torsos, I imagined the delicious contrast between soft hair and hard muscle. I remembered the woodlands I explored as a child, the rich moss I used to stroke, a carpet covering curves of sandstone.

❦

These days, working on a middle-aged crisis that has already spawned two tattoos (each of those spawning an argument with John), I'm looking at motorcycles with a greedy eye. My sister and John are both quietly horrified. They know the accident statistics and quote them regularly.

I was doubly drunk, my first time on a motorcycle, speeding along the road above Bluestone Reservoir. Too much cheap, sweet wine. And that boy's belly. He wore a gray half shirt. He invited me for a ride. I wrapped my hands about his bare waist gingerly, as fearful as Wing Biddlebaum in Sherwood Anderson's "Hands," somehow afraid that something in my touch would give away how excited I was, how aroused, how intoxicated. It is difficult for me, from this distance, to know how momentous that touch felt. As if a stingy God had relented for a brief period and given a few crumbs to the famished.

Emerald Whisperings

I think the field trips for the many biology classes I took to complete my degree in nature interpretation are my favorite undergraduate memories. Ornithology with Dr. Wiley, dendrology with Dr. Guthrie, aquatic seed plants with Dr. Clovis. Instead of hunching over microscopes in laboratories, we forestry majors piled onto a bus and headed out into the countryside. We slogged around Cooper's Rock State Forest in the pouring rain, notebooks and clipboards shielded inside transparent plastic bags, learning about sourwood and chestnut oak. We explored every path in the Core Arboretum, stumbling upon wood ducks and great blue herons, pawpaw thickets and the spring ephemera of bluebells and dog's-tooth violets. I had two great loves those years: flora—the plants I studied in botany classes—and fauna, meaning certain handsome classmates.

Flora

I am still hopelessly enamored of plants. My partner gently mocks me because of my weird and compulsive communing with trees. I touch them. Yes, I literally hug them. I stand before the greatest of them, humble, and I close my eyes and place my palms flat against their bark, trying to imagine the long years they've seen, the weathers they've witnessed. I drive friends mad with my constant appreciative chatter in the woodlands: "See, this here is the spicebush. Smell the leaves. Makes good tea. And this bark! Notice the lenticels in this birch bark." When someone cuts a tree down, I'm furious. When a hard storm uproots a tree, I mourn.

I knew a little bit about botany as a child, walking the woods with my father, his stride so much longer than mine. But it was in those botany classes at WVU that I really became a priest of the woods, poring over my collection of note cards, learning which trees had opposite leaves and which had alternate, learning mellifluous scientific names like *Liquidambar styraciflua*, the sweet gum, and *Amelanchier arborea*, the sarvisberry. How I relished the folktales and the narratives surrounding certain species of trees. For instance, the redbud is called the Judas tree because Judas is said to have hanged himself on such a tree, dyeing the blooms red with his blood guilt. The sarvisberry derived its name from the time of its blooming: about the time mountain thaws would allow the circuit preacher to reach remote areas and hold services for those who had died during the winter. To this day I keep track of the seasons through phenology, the regularly recurring appearance of this or that botanical phenomenon. It is spring when the coltsfoot appears, when the sarvisberry blooms. Summer is almost over when joe-pye weed flowers and ironweed purples the pastures.

Fauna

Those years cruising the Fox and other gay bars, I was intelligent enough to notice that the men I found attractive, the men I emulated, were very like those southern mountain men I'd grown up around, men I'd hungrily studied with that heady combination of fear and desire. This realization was strengthened during my forestry classes in Percival Hall and my biology classes in Brooks Hall, classes abrim with incredibly sexy boys. Most of them were beefily muscular, used to the outdoors. They wore lumberjack boots, jeans, thermal undershirts, baseball caps, and flannel shirts. Most sported beards. The chest hair that had become a prime fetish of mine curled over their T-shirt tops, smoke from a mine fire. Most of them were much like me in their southern upbringing: though they looked gruff, they were often soft-spoken and polite, with mountain or deep-South drawls. Having long ago learned protective coloration, and, more recently, a butch bar persona, I fit right in.

Eventually I began to feel less like a clever imposter and more like a man among men with whom I had much in common. I had always, on one level, been afraid of other men; all my earliest friends, in childhood and adolescence, had been women. My mother, grandmother, and sister had taken care of me. My father, influential as he'd been in many positive ways, was the disciplinarian and thus a source of fear. And I sensed that most of the guys I desired in high school would respond to my admiration with physical violence. But these forestry buddies I felt fairly easy around, though I certainly wasn't yet brave enough to come out to them. One of them, Randy, a married ex-firefighter with a full beard already silvering, became a regular companion. In classes I studied the thick hair on his arms and fantasized about what he would look like after I pulled his shirt off. Amusingly, he thought I was a real stud, because every time he saw me I was with a different woman. "Gigolo," he called me. What he didn't know was that all those women were lesbians.

Being surrounded by so many desirable forestry majors was both frustrating and inspiring. In botany lab, watching Dan spit snuff into a pop can and absent-mindedly give his pen head, I wondered if India ink could be any blacker than his beard. In mammalogy, I tried to memorize the imprint of Kevin's nipples against his WVU Forestry Club T-shirt (the motto on the back: "Foresters Do It in the Woods"). One blissful day, in aquatic seed plants, a course I took with most of my favorite lumberjack look-alikes, the professor took us out to Cheat Lake for lab. It was an early September afternoon, very hot, and the class ended up wading about in the mud looking for plants whose names I've long ago forgotten. What has not escaped my memory is all the doffed T-shirts. Every boy in the class stripped to the waist, including myself, a beginning weight lifter and thus a novice exhibitionist. There, briefly, were all the bare chests I'd fantasized about for semesters. An onanist's dream. I would have settled down in a log cabin on a ridge with any one of them.

Sawdust in Belly Hair

There is a delicious paneroticism in much of Walt Whitman's work. The speaker of the poems often revels in his own body and pushes that body against the body of the world as if, no human partners in the offing, he might take nature as a lover. He rolls in grass, he is licked by waves. It is the exuberant sexuality of the young man whom unaccommodating circumstances have forced into celibacy. Without specific focus, Eros infuses the universe.

The boy's beard is still black, hair is still thick on his head. Unemployed for a year after undergraduate school, he lives with his parents, making sparse money here and there by painting houses. He reads a lot of Whitman, Yeats, and Plath. He drinks cheap beer, watches football, and listens to records by the country music group Alabama. He sleeps alone every night, as men who love men often do in small towns. Today, he has windfall limbs to saw for the fireplace. It is unusually warm for this time of year, the day before the spring equinox. He pulls off his shirt and begins to saw. About him the first tiny signs of returning vegetation fulfill an ancient promise.

For an hour he labors. His armpits grow moist, and he thinks of Whitman: "The scent of these arm-pits aroma finer than prayer." Finished, he carries armloads of wood to the shed, then pops open a beer for lunch and brushes sawdust from his belly. After years of secretly admiring the hairy bodies of men, he finds his own adolescent body maturing. With pleasure and pride, he strokes the sparse fur on his chest and belly with his fingertips. Most days, it feels as if he is wasting his youth here at home, squandering his passion in his own hand. His, after all, is the only young man's body available to savor. His is an insular narcissism born of necessity.

Still, today, the beer tastes good, and the japonica's tiny new leaves give him hope. One day soon, he will take the train out of here and find many amours in many cities, men who will touch him the way today he touches himself. He will never return to this hateful town, this cultural wasteland.

Meanwhile, there is this sunny day, the enviable contentment of the cat, and this waxing sun, spreading its warmth on his shoulders and back like the hands of a lover.

Two

Gathering Green Tomatoes in the Rain

Anyone who knows me knows
I've waited years for this—
sleeping late on Sundays with a man
so kind I'm suspicious, as I was

all over Ireland, where the solicitude
of strangers made me fear a mugging
waited around the corner of each hospitable
word. I curl for hours against your back,

its soft larch-bough wings of fur,
I curl into the rain's incessance, that first
steady autumn rain, summer's sodden
funeral. Almost noon when we rise.

"Fried-green-tomato weather,"
I announce, that southern delicacy
I have promised you for weeks.
"Are they breakfast food?" you wonder,

and now we are huddled together
by your stoop-side garden, beneath
your huge cathedral-arch
umbrella, temporary oasis of dry,

feeling the hemisphere slope its slow
day-by-day away from the light.
I am bending and cupping firm
unripe jade stippled with storm,

retreating to the kitchen, slicing them,
coring out the tough bit of pithy white.
"The secret ingredient," I announce,
hillbilly hierophant, taking down

the sugar bowl, mixing that touch
of sweet with cornmeal, salt, pepper,

heating up the sine que non of
southern cooking, bacon grease,

easing the dusted tomatoes in,
frying the coating a crackling
gold-brown. Perfect with Tabasco,
with the mozzarella-and-fresh-basil

omelette you fry up, the melon
you slice. Grinning, we gobble
every bite. All the years
before—giving, giving, gifts

to those who could not care,
would not give back.
How well we make a feast together.
Those years of waste are over.

A Red-Gold Mustache

All summer I watched him. His name was Steve, and he was a bartender at the Double Decker's downstairs bar, which on Friday and Saturday nights catered to gays and lesbians. He wore clothes that showed off his lean waist, big chest, and curvaceous ass. When he washed glasses, I stared at the veins cresting the pale, thick curves of his biceps. I wanted to feel his red-gold mustache against my black beard.

It was 1982, the summer before I began graduate school at WVU. I was exceedingly poor, working at a meaningless part-time job, but I preferred to be destitute and among gay friends in Morgantown than to be isolated among the homophobes in Hinton. In the evenings, with little else to do, I headed down the humid streets to drink cheap beer at the Double Decker and to study Steve. I watched his fine form gyrating to Chubby Checker's "The Twist" during a work break or mixing up Long Island iced teas for customers and thought he was the most desirable man I'd ever seen. His good looks intimidated me: it was hard to keep my voice steady when I asked him for a Miller Lite. I had had little luck with men before, and my self-image was pretty low, so I couldn't imagine getting lucky enough to lure him home. In fact, I couldn't imagine being brave enough even to ask him to dance.

Somehow I did. Somehow we ended up on the dance floor, dancing close. I rode home with him in his Opal. He dallied with me for a few weeks. Then he lost interest and moved on to the slew of other admirers his good looks attracted. He moved to Florida that fall, and in his aftermath I saw the color of his hair in sunsets, in the crimson of October maple leaves and Boston ivy.

Steve was handsome and promiscuous in the early 1980s, at a time when none of us knew what virus was spreading across America. I wonder if he is still alive today. I doubt it. In the autumn I think of him sometimes, when the maple leaves turn red beyond my bedroom window. Over twenty years later, I want to thank him for sharing, however briefly, his pale and muscled body, his warmth, the scratchy kisses of his red-gold mustache with a shy kid whose greatest dream was to touch beauty, and who, for a few blessed candlelit nights, did.

Remember This Healing

I don't think about him much, the man I mooned over in graduate school. Paul was a broad-shouldered, handsome, smooth-talking, charming sort, the kind of man I am always attracted to and now recognize as very dangerous. Vee and Laura, mutual friends, introduced us in the fall of 1982. Paul and his lover, Rod, had me over for brunch once, and I was impressed with the cheese-grits casserole, the home-canned hot peppers, Paul's beefy torso discernible beneath his Polo shirt, and his muscular, hairy forearms. One weekend Vee and Laura, Paul and Rod, and I (perpetual fifth wheel) went to a Japanese steak house in Pittsburgh and then out to the bars. I thought that Paul was just what I was looking for, but, of course—just my luck—he already had a spouse.

Then one cold night, January of 1983, Paul showed up at the Double Decker with the news that he and Rod had gone their separate ways. Secretly delighted, I was full of consolation and sympathy. Paul grew flirtatious and affectionate, and soon we were both drunk on gin and tonics and dancing close. By the end of the evening, we were making liquor-dulled love in my tiny studio apartment by the light of an oil lamp, and sleet was clicking on the windowpanes. When he grinned at me in the flickering light—so much resembling the young Hemingway—crossed his ankles in the small of my back and brushed my mustache with his, we both knew I was hooked.

He teased me for almost a year. I sent him hopeful bouquets of roses, I bought him presents, I wrote passionate poems that eventually ended up in my master's thesis. He reconciled with Rod, broke up with Rod again, came over to my place for drinks, flirted and led me on, then took up with yet another man, a man with a fine house and inherited money. He stood me up several times. I recall one absolutely agonizing evening waiting for the sound of his car, lying on the floor of my apartment and trying to read Faulkner's *The Sound and the Fury*, realizing once midnight arrived that Paul wasn't going to show up.

In March of 1983, he had a health scare. A growth in his throat, something that might have been cancer. During his hospital stay, I brought wine, roses, Cadbury Easter eggs (a favorite of his), chicken burritos, all of which involved long walks across town, since I had no car. I waited for him during his surgery, only to be accosted by Rod, who showed up to ask what my intentions were. I rejoiced with Paul when the news came: just a problem with the thyroid gland. Somehow the bandage at his throat made him even more precious to me, highlighting as it did his mortality and how I might have lost him. Watching him sleep, I stroked his hairy forearms. I sniffed the red roses I'd brought, scribbled notes for a poem—of praise, of thanks, something to detain the day—then stared out the window at the tiny white crosses of a pauper's graveyard across the valley. Soon the spring equinox would arrive, and the first coltsfoot blooms would spring up along the country roads of Monongalia County.

Wintry Woods

I remember the despair, running across Steve toward summer's end, as he and his thick-muscled new boyfriend exited the Great Wall of China Restaurant. I was on the outside again: not in his arms, reverencing his nakedness in candlelight, but walking down dark Morgantown streets and through dark Morgantown neighborhoods, looking enviously at lit windows and wondering how happier folks spent their evenings.

I remember clearly the sick sense in my stomach when I discovered that Jack, only a few weeks after dumping me, had taken up with a bucktoothed queen from Beckley. I remember my nausea, hearing that Paul was moving in with his wealthy new lover. And, more recently, a mere decade ago, I remember that final manipulative e-mail message from Thomas, his attempt to lure me back into a cul-de-sac relationship by describing how good his new leather jacket looked with his dark beard and hairy torso.

On some subconscious level, perhaps I chose those men not only for their desirability but for their inaccessibility. Certainly my therapists have said so. Perhaps I was looking for drama and conflict, poetry fodder, intensity and not true intimacy. What I got, along with several good poems, was dashed hopes and deepened loneliness. I did not ever seriously contemplate suicide—unlike so many harassed, frightened, and cornered gays and lesbians. Alcohol overuse, drug abuse, and suicide are unusually high in the gay and lesbian community because of the many societal pressures we face. Still, I casually thought, driving back roads home after reading Thomas's final e-mail, mesmerized by the fall of snow on my windshield, how easy it would be to keep the truck straight on one of the curves between Ballard and Forest Hill and embed myself in a mountainside.

Suicide is an act, a temptation, I well understand. It is a way to stop pain you think will end no other way. But, short of mortal illness or a police standoff, suicide is no longer an exit I would take. It is one of the advantages of age to know that almost every pain passes, or at least dwindles to a point at which it can be borne.

41

Two Lovers

Sometimes it feels as if my Appalachian roots and my desire for men are two lovers I vacillate between. When I feel spurned by one, I take up with the other.

How badly I wanted to leave the mountains once I realized I was gay and took up my shy pursuit of men. Even after I'd made it to Morgantown and discovered the gay community there, what I wanted was to join the distant urban fray. The novels I read in college—John Rechy's *The Sexual Outlaw*, Andrew Holleran's *Dancer from the Dance*, Edmund White's *Nocturnes for the King of Naples*, Patricia Nell Warren's *The Beauty Queen*—were all set in big cities, full of enticing bars, handsome men, and lots of sex. Nothing at all like Appalachia, where many physically and emotionally isolated gays and lesbians sometimes drive for hours down back roads to get to that smoky, dark bar in Morgantown, Charleston, Bluefield, or Huntington just to spend time with other gay folks. My undergraduate friends Allen and Robin took Appalachian literature at WVU and enthusiastically mentioned this and that mountain writer to me, but, at that point in my life, I had no interest in the topic. Appalachia was a place where it was hard to be honest, where my lesbian friends and I had been attacked and insulted. I wanted to put such a backward place behind me.

So I turned my back on my native landscape—beautiful prison, so it felt. When I made my hopeful move to Washington, DC, I rented a room from Philip, a gay vocal coach whose roots were also West Virginian, a warm, funny man who treated me like an old friend from the moment we met in a crowded bar in Dupont Circle, DC's gay neighborhood. We lived out in the Maryland suburbs, in Fort Washington. I had no car and so rode the commuter bus into the city to teach part-time for George Washington University. I met a few men through Philip, who had contacts in DC's Gay Men's Chorus, but no reciprocal fires sprang up. I was intimidated by the big city, and without my own transportation, stuck in the suburbs, I couldn't become the predatory bar fly I'd hoped to become. Some men—more confident, more charismatic—might do well in the urban hunt for love, but not this quiet, less-than-gorgeous, less-than-charming country boy. To my horror, I found myself homesick, hating the concrete and the cars, missing the mountains, missing even my father's vegetable gardens, which I'd resentfully helped him tend for years. One night I heard John Denver's "Take Me Home, Country Roads" on the radio and grew so misty eyed I couldn't help but laugh at my own sentimentality.

When I did return to Appalachia, broke and unemployed, I felt like the gay world had betrayed me. A few months with my family in Hinton, a few years teaching English at WVU, a few failed attempts at romance, then a better job nearer home in Blacksburg, Virginia. In the early 1990s, Elizabeth Fine, at that time head of Virginia Tech's Appalachian Studies Program, invited me to teach Introduction to Appalachian Studies, and that proved to be a turning point in my self-definition and my attitude toward my native region.

How well you learn what you teach. I discovered the long, painful history of Appalachia, the depth of its folk culture, the breadth of its writers. I took up with other folks in my department with accents similar to my own, especially Alice Kinder, whose country-bred warmth, humor, and kindness made me look at my own long-neglected background in a new light. I started calling myself a hillbilly, half jokingly, half proudly. When I heard that, behind my back, a friend's homophobic boyfriend had referred to me as a "rump-ranger," I began to joke about wearing a T-shirt slogan that would sum up my dual identity: "Ridge-Runner Rump-Ranger."

Local students in my Appalachian studies classes helped catalyze this transformation too. The stories they told of the mockery they'd suffered enraged me: jokes about their accents, their clothing, not only from classmates but even from professors. The students, in turn, warmed up to me fast, recognizing me as a mountain brother by my accent and by the family anecdotes I used as illustrations in lectures. Excited to have a teacher who honored their heritage, a teacher who waxed ecstatic over mountain cooking, my generous students brought me homegrown or home-canned treat after treat. A jar of kudzu jelly, deer jerky, moonshine (always shyly presented after class), creecy greens, corn relish. Even the notorious wild onion: a paper bag full of fresh ramps. The perquisites of an Appalachian studies instructor!

Eventually, instead of feeling like a queer oppressed by redneck Appalachians, I began to see the oppression that Appalachians and homosexuals have in common. Clear enough, when you start to count all the queer jokes and hillbilly/West Virginia jokes you've heard.

Sunset over Hinton

What kind of life would I have lived had I stayed in my hometown? It's a moot point, because there are few jobs in that area, certainly none in my field, but still I wonder.

Before I met John, first as a student and then as an instructor at WVU and later as a teacher at Virginia Tech, I spent summers and school breaks in Hinton. It was good to spend time at home, to get a lot of reading done and home cooking devoured. The grass cutting got to be tiresome, and I never much liked picking strawberries, but other garden chores were fairly pleasant, at least as research for poems, and for a time I got to be semicompetent with an ax.

But as fond as I have always been of my family, and as open with them as I was even then about my true nature, I often thought of a line from a Bette Midler song during those extended visits home: "Nobody knows me, I've got no reason to stay." My gay friends were in Blacksburg or Morgantown, and the nearest gay bar was in Bluefield, a friendly but shabby place I didn't think was worth the drive. Once in a while, I would stay over with my friend Allen in Stanaford, and we'd drive down the West Virginia Turnpike to Charleston's Grand Palace to dance and watch the gaggles of big-haired drag queens. Ever so rarely, my Beckley buddy Jim would come down for some late-night dalliance. Other than that, I had a taste of the isolation I would have been swallowed by had I stayed in Hinton. I read a lot, I watched a lot of television. Always, at the end of the academic break, I was ready to go back to Morgantown or Blacksburg. A man needs to be around his own kind. For queer Appalachians, family is of monumental importance, but it is not enough.

❦

Gays and lesbians must make themselves. None of us are brought up prepared to be gay. What did I know of homosexuality before I met Jo Davison and read *The Front Runner?*

My first big trip out west. I'm twelve and ready to accompany Nanny and Poppy to Grand Junction, Colorado, to visit Nanny's brother Harry. My mother sees fit to warn me about certain men who might get fresh with me in public restrooms. (That would be one desperate man, to hungrily approach the acne-stippled, pudgy adolescent I was.) "Just knee them in the groin," she advises, "and then run."

My father is listening to my grandmother play piano in the living room. "I used to play piano pretty well," he muses, "before the war. My first piano teacher made a pass at me. I never went back."

Someone in junior high tells me that Rock Hudson and Jim Nabors are getting married. "That can't be," I think, thoroughly confused. "Two men can't get married."

Playground gossip has it that the slender and effeminate son of a certain teacher has been caught in a compromising position in the movie-house restroom with a fat, retarded kid who's the regular brunt of high-school mockery. I have no idea what shameful things two boys could do together. I am very young and have been carefully sheltered. My imagination is very, very limited.

An ecology club cookout at the roadside park, just the other side of the Bluestone River Bridge. Too much lemonade, so I head for the bathroom. There, scrawled on the walls, Summers County gay history. Invitations, certain measurements, a sketch or two. A phone number, a suggested date and time to meet. Desperate attempts at connection in a wasteland, made sordid by secrecy. "FAG!" someone else has inked into the wood as critical commentary.

The late 1980s. This winter afternoon my college friend Cindy has joined me in Hinton for a visit, and she and I are walking past the Summers County Courthouse, a huge red-brick turreted structure. I look like I usually do: beard, jeans, lumberjack boots, black leather jacket. She is more anomalous in this context, for she is dressed pretty much the same as I, with the addition of one of those short haircuts the lesbian community favors. Women in Summers County do not dress like this.

A pickup truck passes us. A guy yells, "Go back where you came from!"

I am no longer that defenseless pacifist from high school. I am a pissed-off queer. Without missing a beat, I shout, "*Fuck* you!" and flip them the accompanying gesture. Cindy and I are ready to tear off some body parts. However, unlike on that night years ago when I got my face punched, the truck does not stop and eject pissed-off rednecks. Instead, it continues on down the street.

I turn to Cindy, laugh, then, with mock pathos, wail, "I *am* where I came from!"

Had I remained there I would have needed a black belt or a bodyguard. I would have withered with isolation and loneliness. I could not stay, but I have not gone far.

Incandescence

Thomas Wolfe understood the sound of a train, and the way hill dwellers, as much as they might cherish home, dream of a new life in the great world beyond the mountains. Always that tension between the urge to leave and the urge to stay.

I read Wolfe's novels in the mid-1980s. In fact, I started *Look Homeward, Angel* in the fall of 1985, that semester when I'd left home and tried to make a new life in the DC area. At that point in my life, the title seemed especially evocative to me, as did Wolfe's description of the poetic suggestiveness of a train whistle echoing down a mountain valley, leading his protagonists to yearn for the long Whitmanesque widths of America.

Rail is one of very few ways to enter and to escape my hometown. To this day, despite financial cutbacks, an Amtrak passenger train stops in Hinton at least twice a week. Hinton's railroad depot, from which I took the train to DC and to which, on the train, I returned, is a solid brick building, full of interesting architectural features. It isn't far from my family's house—in fact, the New River, the train station, and the railroad track are just over the side of the hill.

Why did I think it was simple, that I would either stay or leave? That I had to choose either Hinton or the world? Now, when I go home, when I lie in bed at night, beneath the bear-claw quilt my Aunt Doris made, I listen to the New River's shushing rapids and the sound of the train moving down the valley, and I know that I will always leave, and I will always return.

❧

Perhaps it's a youthful mirage, the belief that some destination or some person awaits that will free us from the banal, the quotidian, the mundane, and make our lives incandescent, burning up the moderate and the wearily habitual. For a while, in my younger days, novelty did that—new places, new men. The beach at Provincetown. First glimpse of San Francisco's towers across the bay. Paul, Jim, Thomas. The bonfire of Eros.

It is so difficult to meet other gay people in small towns and rural areas, though the Internet has made it infinitely easier than it was when I was a lonely bachelor in Hinton, Morgantown, or Blacksburg. When I try to imagine gay folks living out their lives in small towns across not only Appalachia but the world, I grow sick with empathy.

Celibacy gives touch an almost religious depth and significance that I, happily coupled, can remember but no longer feel. For so many years, unable to meet other men with any ease, I made of sexuality a kind of shrine. To touch a beautiful man was one entrance into a sense of the divine. My neopagan beliefs only encourage this attitude: deity is not transcendent—a detached force located in some distant heavenly realm—but immanent—present in natural phenomena, the human body, and sensual delight. Thus, in "The Charge of the Goddess," one of modern Wicca's most poetic manifestos, the Moon Goddess says, "All acts of love and pleasure are my rituals." No wonder many gays and lesbians are attracted to such a flesh-positive faith, rather than to Christianity, which so often takes patriarchal and flesh-hating forms.

❦

I met Jim in a gay bar in Beckley, West Virginia, one snowy night. Nothing romantic was to develop, but the sexual connection was intense enough to satisfy. His mother was an overprotective harpy, so, on the nights he would come to visit me in Hinton, during those summers and school breaks I spent at home in the mid-1980s, he would wait till she called him to see that he was ready for bed, then he would head down Beckley Mountain in the winding dark. I would wait for him in the tree-lined park outside my family's house, backpack full of ropes, lube, condoms, and bandanas. He would arrive a little bit before midnight with a thermos of Scotch and 7-Up, and we would retire to my father's empty farmhouse up in the country at Forest Hill. Off would come the T-shirts, the boots, and the jeans. I loved his beard, his gym-hard body, his thick West Virginia accent. I loved to lie there afterward, listening to the crickets, cool night air wafting the window curtains.

One early spring night, he dropped me off back in Hinton about four in the morning. I stood on the street, his scent still on my fingers. On the great wall of mountain, across the New River from the town, two strips of forest fire blazed in the darkness, as if some deity of fire had written his initials into the steep side of awakening earth.

Displaced Seeds

I love country music. Many of my queer big-city brethren would no doubt be horrified by this confession, but then they wouldn't be impressed with my harness-strap boots, thermal undershirts, and four-by-four pickup truck either. When I'm driving that pickup—and there's nothing I like better than driving Appalachian back roads, with no one before me and no one behind me—I always listen to country music. There are Tim McGraw, one of the sexiest men alive (yes, I like his voice too); Brooks and Dunn (what a handsome couple they'd make); Mary Chapin Carpenter (a true poet); Toby Keith (hot bear, great baritone, disappointingly conservative politics). But just about my favorite is Kathy Mattea, who hails from Cross Lanes, West Virginia, and just about my favorite song of hers is "Seeds," written by Pat Alger and Ralph Murphy. Every time I hear it, the song's dominant metaphor seizes me: we're "all just seeds in God's hands." Is it divine will or chance that determines whether those seeds land on rich earth or inhospitable sand?

When I decided to study both literature and forestry during my WVU undergraduate days, perhaps even then I was unconsciously trying to balance the refined and the rough in my nature, the indoors and the outdoors, the educated queer and the woodland-tramping hillbilly. One thing I remember learning in one of many well-taught botany classes was the definition of a weed: any plant that's growing where it's not wanted. Thus, in a tobacco patch, even a rose would be a weed.

Sometimes we crucify ourselves. Some saboteur inside of us chooses wrongly, colludes with circumstance.

Before John, there was another. A desirable, complex, fascinating man who was already spoken for. A man who met me for afternoon trysts nevertheless, in a borrowed A-frame in the woods outside Blacksburg, Virginia. I loved Thomas passionately and—if one defines health as moderation—unhealthily, for there was nothing moderate about what I felt. Like a medieval troubadour attached to an inaccessible married woman, I wrote poem after poem. I lived at a depth of feeling I will probably never experience again.

I met Thomas in February of 1991, just about the time the mourning dove begins to call its sad tripartite song from tree limb and gable. A mutual friend introduced us over the bench press in Virginia Tech's War Memorial Gym. I was fascinated. I'd been single and celibate for a long time, and Thomas was just my type: short, muscular, hairy, and exceedingly intelligent.

We had many interests in common, including neopaganism and the occult. We met at his townhouse on Huntington Lane in the late afternoons, drank coffee, and talked: about Aleister Crowley, the Order of the Golden Dawn, elementals, and Enochian magic. On the spring equinox, he brought me a tiny new larch cone and a "Happy Equinox" card, relics I have still.

I knew he had a long-term boyfriend, a man I honestly liked. But I fell in love anyway. Thomas was the most erotic man I'd ever gotten close to. Here was my chance to burn with that hard, gemlike flame Walter Pater spoke about in my Victorian literature anthology, and I didn't care about the consequences. I wasn't concerned with morality. It was intensity that demanded my devotion.

Both Thomas and his lover, Dick, were planning to leave Blacksburg in September, after Thomas finished his master's degree and he and Dick found jobs in the wider world. With our time together circumscribed both by the narrow limits of adultery and by this upcoming end-of-summer departure, I was determined to enjoy such a tumultuous passion while I could. For the first time in my life, it felt as if a man I loved might actually reciprocate that feeling. And, already in my early thirties, I had enough of a sense of mortality to know that such ardor might not come again any time soon, if ever.

Does scarcity encourage us to make bad choices? So said my last therapist, one to whom my feelings for Thomas drove me, and I well know how scarce are romantic options for many gays in small-town and rural

America. Falling in love with a man already partnered is not a choice I am likely to make again. My reasons are practical, not ethical: I am no longer willing to live with the likely consequences. But it is not a choice I regret, despite the eventual heartbreak. I lived to the fullest one of the greatest passions of my life. There is something both foolish and heroic about that.

Thomas, in July of 1991, had a horticultural conference to attend in State College, Pennsylvania. He told Dick that he was riding up with other graduate students, but instead he rode up with me. On the way, we stopped in Washington, DC, for a few nights, staying with my friend Cindy. I wanted to show this handsome satyr off to my urban friends.

Adultery is hard on all involved. Thomas seemed to enjoy having a new person on the side, someone for whom he was novel and fascinating, someone who made love to him with astonished reverence and endless invention, but he was willing to risk only so much. Finally, after months of stealing a few hours together in the afternoons, always checking our wristwatches, finally, in Cindy's guest bed, we got to spend the night together. I was ready to devour him. Yet after lovemaking, he seemed impatient with my afterglow caresses and soon turned his back on me. The distance, physical and emotional, maddened me.

Comfortably coupled a decade later, now I understand his yearning for some flame marriage does not encourage, his caution in the face of an intimacy that might wreck his life, his fear that he might lose everything he knew and trusted and be left with an emotionally erratic, perfervid poet. But then I did not understand. I knew only that he was everything to me and that I wanted more. More lovemaking, more time with him, more affection and emotional openness, some kind of solid promise I could grasp. To his credit, he made no empty promises. A consummate liar, he refused to lie on that score. He did say "I love you," but to this day I have no idea whether that was a lie or not.

Icefall

With over a decade's distance, I have turned agony into self-deprecating humor. I have made a hyperbolic joke of that terrible parting, that worst of all pains to date. I call it "The Apocalyptic Divergence." Spring break 1992. Those five days in Framingham, Massachusetts, visiting Thomas and his partner, Dick. Breaking it off with Thomas and driving home alone.

I am no good with numbers. I have a problem remembering birth dates and phone numbers, but I remember Thursday, September 19, 1991, the day that Thomas came by my office with the news I'd been dreading all summer. Dick had been offered a job at a Borders bookstore in Massachusetts, and so they would be leaving Blacksburg in just a few days. I put my head in his lap and cried. Unusual for me—I try to save tears for a space without witnesses. For the first time, I told him I loved him, and, to my shock, he replied in kind. I walked him to the front steps of my office building, we shook hands—I believe, even in that extremity, he seductively tickled my palm with his forefinger—and then I watched his form dwindle with distance. The scent of juniper was thick in the end-of-summer heat. He disappeared behind a building. I stepped back into Williams Hall, just in time for my late-afternoon freshman composition class. I taught that class with my sunglasses on.

There was no way I would have the emotional composure to help them load up the moving van, though Dick might reasonably expect me to pitch in, along with all their other Blacksburg friends, since he knew nothing of the agony their imminent departure was arousing in me. So I claimed that my friend Cindy had a crisis in DC and drove there for a long weekend, listening to Nanci Griffith on the tape deck, my glasses spotting with salt like melting winter roads. I spent several days with her, in a state of despair the likes of which I've never suffered since. Cindy took me out to Cleveland Park's ethnic restaurants, bought me beers, drove me up to Baltimore for brunch at an old college friend's house, and took me for walks down tree-lined streets.

It was the sort of pain, in retrospect, that proves valuable. Go through a loss like that, and, the rest of your life, when faced with hardship, you can look back at that dark chasm and say, "If I could survive that, I can survive anything."

My affair with Thomas continued via scrawled, lengthy, erotic letters. I sent him photocopied poems by Robert Lowell and W. B. Yeats. He sent me a pentagram ring for the Celtic Samhain festival, to my utter amazement: talk about keeping me on the hook. For Valentine's Day he sent me a tiny, bright-red bear with horns and devil's tail. On the bear's shirt were printed the words "I love you." The ring and the bear are in a cardboard box in my father's house in Hinton, along with all Thomas's letters. Things I do not want to see again, but things I cannot entirely part with. I do not want to relive history, but I cling to its debris with a stubborn grip. Certainly poems do that: pointed attempts to remember what shapes us. River-smoothed stones along the banks of the Greenbrier. The asymmetrical forms of Dolly Sod's wind-flagged spruce.

Thomas and Dick invited me to visit during my spring break, and so I made the long drive up, stopping at New Market Battlefield and at Cindy's DC apartment to break up the trip. Right off the Massachusetts Turnpike, there it was, Framingham's Borders Bookstore, where they now were both employed. Within five minutes, I'd found Thomas stocking shelves. Within ten minutes, Dick had appeared and given me a big hug.

Those days return in shards. A Boston leather bar—Thomas dancing in the tight black T-shirt and jeans I always found him so irresistible in. Trying to keep my hands off him, trying to give Dick no basis for suspicion. A day trip into Boston, where I bought a ceramic Pan, still on my Blacksburg altar, and a Medusa head I gave to Thomas later that week, when I decided the affair had to end. (Have the courage to face facts, even if they turn you to stone.) A trip to Walden Pond. Hours of stolen lovemaking while Dick was at work—on the bed, on the couch, before a mirror. Thomas's hands bound behind his back, his furry nipples in my mouth.

That last day together. Cold New England wind. Violet skies, a few snow-flurries. Naked on the couch, the warmth of his body, the thick dark fur I so relished covering his chest and belly. Then not naked. Putting on the layers, mustering what few self-protective instincts I had left. Telling him I could continue our connection no longer. Too painful. Crumbs compared to the kind of relationship I wanted with him.

Dick home a little after five. My careful composure, the wonderful power of southerners to put on a false face. Pizza, beer, a rented movie. Dick making some comment about love being like fire: it always leaves a telltale smoke. He was a very intelligent man. Perhaps even then he knew.

Thomas, with unusual solicitude, made up a bed for me on the couch. They retired to their bedroom together and closed the door behind them. I lay in the dark and stared at the ceiling, listened to the wind and the cars out on the turnpike. In the morning, I woke very early. I packed. I tapped on their bedroom door. Invited in, I sat on the edge of the bed. Dick shirtless: pale, lean, torso dusted with a little hair. Thomas wearing a dark T-shirt, the outlines of his muscular chest visible against the cloth. I kissed Dick's brow, then Thomas's, and I left.

All along the turnpike, cascades of ice, the shape of stalactites clinging to the roadside rocks. Another romantic failure, another flight back to Appalachia. I stopped in at a Friendly's, a chain I'd never heard of before. I ordered a big meal, and, as I sat there, lonelier than I've ever been, before or since, I realized how grateful I was, in the midst of a large-scale emotional disaster, to have small pleasures to anticipate. The adult is concerned with grand desires—love, success, freedom— but the child takes delight in country-fried steak and lots of gravy to sop up with biscuits. Sometimes it is the love for such small things that keeps us from suicide.

Bodies We Have Loved

"*There's always someone haunting someone*," sings Carly Simon on her superb album *Boys in the Trees*, one of my undergraduate favorites. She is a songwriter who has meticulously delineated the complexities, ambiguities, comedies, and tragedies of the human heart. Carly, I would be more than glad to buy you a lobster dinner and a fine bottle of wine in some upscale Martha's Vineyard restaurant, then sip bourbon on your deck, watch fireflies drift in, and compare romantic joys and foibles till well after midnight.

After parting with men I have loved—Steve, Paul, Thomas—for years, even decades afterward I have seen traces of them everywhere. As if they have diffused into the world, like incense smoke, like milkweed seeds, silver unspooling down the wind. Without the body of a beloved to touch, one learns to love the body of nature, to reach the past, make sense of it, through the present. In other words, and obviously, one's emotional history shapes the way one views the world, makes the details of landscape into metaphor. Poems often serve as a way of articulating that double vision, that unasked-for grace, the conjunction of the inner world and the outer that deepens the significance of both.

So, Steve, in the autumnal red of Boston ivy. Paul, in spring's last snowbanks. Thomas, in the soft, new, green needles of the larch.

Sometimes I dream about Thomas, author of my greatest devastation, even now, in the midst of my *optima dies*. "Optima dies prima fugit," said Virgil. "The best day flees first." The most ardor-drenched days flee first, perhaps, but they are not always the best. They are perhaps the most memorable.

My friend Cindy broke up with her girlfriend Susan at about the same time that Thomas and I parted ways, and, during those bleak days in the early 1990s, we used to commiserate about how badly used we felt, how haunted, and how inescapable the past seemed to be. Ambushes, Cindy called them—those little reminders of what's lost that blindside you constantly. I seemed to see Thomas's face, his brow, his physique, everywhere, and every reminder brought a stab of pain. Short, muscular men passing me on a campus sidewalk; late-afternoon beard stubble; a Borders bookstore advertisement; the gym where we met; the duck pond where we used to walk together; the coo of a mourning dove. All of it maddened me.

If I had ever become an alcoholic, it would have been then, those months after my trip to Framingham and the break-up with Thomas. I spent late nights with Jane at the Cellar, drinking pitchers of cheap Olympia beer. I spent afternoons in the Underground, drinking ale after ale, aching, watching my handsome straight buddy Jim throw darts and wondering what it was in me that fell for the wrong men again and again, wondering what profound flaw of my heart, mind, or body kept Thomas from giving himself to me completely. When spring came again, I hated it. I detested the crocuses and the violets, the new green on the larch trees. It was a rebirth I was denied, locked out of. I wanted autumn—the fiery self-immolation of the sugar maples—or winter—blessed numbness.

Rotting Crab Apples

It was the emotional waste that tormented me. For Cindy and I to spend so much emotional currency on Susan and Thomas for so long, only to end up with nothing—it seemed like intolerable injustice. We were bright, well-educated, passionate, and attractive, yet suddenly we found ourselves completely devoid of romantic possibilities. In my case, living in Blacksburg—a town without a gay bar and with few social opportunities for gay people—was a real handicap. In Cindy's case, living in DC didn't help. Occasionally, during my visits to DC, Cindy and I would walk down Connecticut Avenue, make note of a particularly ill-favored person, and observe with our characteristic mixture of self-pity, sharp irony, and sheer bitchiness: "I'll bet that troll has someone waiting at home for him. Unlike ourselves!" Our gifts were like acorns fallen on asphalt, or fruit unharvested. We were, to borrow the southern phrase used to describe pathetic bachelors and spinsters, like wine grapes "dyin' on the vine."

❦

In bleak moods, I love bleak landscapes. "What good is desire?" I thought, walking my father's farm, through the stubbly cornfields of late winter, soon after my return from Massachusetts and the breakup with Thomas. Desire opens you up to heartbreak, disappointment, frustration, and attack. It makes you hope and ache for what can't be had. It makes life without the desired object hardly worth living. In the case of gays, desire emphasizes your difference. It makes you think about jumping off bridges or driving into hillsides.

I couldn't have Steve, I couldn't have Paul, I couldn't have Thomas. Where in my readings of the existentialists did I encounter it, the idea that hope is not a gift but the last and worse curse that Pandora freed? The odds are against us sexual minorities. We are one in ten, if that. What's the likelihood that a man I am attracted to at the gym will be equally attracted to me? In those bitter bachelor days, I used to sing Joni

59

Mitchell's "The Last Time I Saw Richard" under my breath a lot: "All romantics meet the same fate someday / cynical and drunk and boring someone in some dark café."

What good is desire without an outlet? It is fine fuel for poems. Is it too much to ask, then, to be both artistically productive and emotionally fulfilled? Are the two states mutually exclusive? Maybe, I thought, as I reached the edge of the cornfield and a sudden snow flurry began, with all my literary ambitions I should keep falling in love with bastards.

Heart's Famine

First there was the Ferrell coat of arms on my grandmother's living-room wall, with the faded typescript on the back detailing the origins of our family in Longford, Ireland. Then there was the poetry of W. B. Yeats one autumn at West Virginia University in Robert Clark's wonderful Survey of English Literature class. There was my first Irish cookbook, in 1989, my way of trying to get back to my European roots, though I couldn't yet afford to actually travel there.

Finally, after a study abroad program I assisted with in summer 1994, there were two weeks in Ireland. Swilling Guinness in Dublin and cruising the gay bathhouse; meeting relatives two hundred years removed in Longford; spending a sweaty night with a handsome, auburn-bearded man I met in a gay bar in Cork; standing on the Cliffs of Moher and within the walls of Dun Aengus; visiting Yeats's grave in Drumcliff. All over the island I saw wrecked and crumbling houses, some ruined since the potato famine, some emptied more recently by the chronic unemployment from which the nation suffers. I was reminded of the coalfields of Appalachia: empty storefronts, jobless residents, abandoned homes.

Late March 1991. Living in Terrace View, one of the soulless apartment complexes that have cropped up like patches of toadstools throughout Blacksburg. Just back from Framingham, from saying goodbye to Thomas. Sleet on the windowpane, freezing on the hemlock tree outside the kitchen window. Tonight, since there is no one to care for me, I will take care of myself. I have Billy Ray Cyrus and Billy Dean, good-looking men to keep me company via Country Music Television. There is a bottle of Bushmills Irish whiskey from which to pour a dram or two. And in Malachi McCormick's *Irish Country Cooking*, there is a recipe I have always wanted to make: Dublin Coddle, a sort of stew with ham, sausages, potatoes, and onions. From a paper bag I pull a few of the last potatoes from my father's garden, and I watch the sleet come down as I cut the eyes from the potatoes. The whiskey warms me. After all my Irish ancestors survived—invasion, warfare, famine—the least I can do is survive a misspent love affair. Endurance—it's a form of heroism small enough to fit into the daily.

Waiting for Crocuses and Silver-Maple Bloom

For a long time, travel was a way to escape what I felt about Thomas. For six months of my life, meeting him was a source of bliss, and being without him was a source of misery. When he and his spouse left town, I needed to remind myself that I could find consolation at the least, joy at the most, without him.

In 1991, while Thomas still lived in Blacksburg, I escaped the tensions of our adulterous relationship by taking a Globus tour to Germany. There, I admired Munich's Frauenkirche and Berlin's Brandenburg Gate and reveled in beer gardens and pastry shops, my oral fixation consigned to roast pork and Black Forest cherry cake rather than illicit lovemaking. I loved the castles lining the Rhine, the firs of the Black Forest, and the ornate palace of King Ludwig II, Linderhof, where I'm sure he hankered painfully, ridden with Catholic guilt, over handsome servants and stable boys.

In 1992, I visited Kevin, a Fulbright scholar friend in Thessaloniki, where every night we would relish tentacles of some sort (cuttlefish, squid, and octopus), split a bottle of retsina, then start in on the ouzo. After a week with him, I took a remarkably inexpensive cruise of the Greek islands, wandering through the streets of Mykonos and Patmos, finally getting to visit the palace of Knossos on Crete. Then a tour of the Greek mainland, where this amateur classics buff saw the Theater of Dionysus, the Acropolis, Corinth, and Delphi. I knew enough about classical Greek attitudes toward homosexuality to feel somewhat at home there, but when I visited one supposed gay bar in Athens, the semiotics of a foreign country were such that I couldn't tell if the place were really gay or not. It did seem clear to me, one afternoon near the Temple of Zeus, that a black-mustached stranger was inviting me into the ruins for a romp, an exciting possibility my small-town caution made me refuse.

In 1993, I took a tour of Austria and Switzerland. This trip proved to be especially pleasant, since an elderly gay couple was part of the crew, and within a day, accurate gaydar had made us buddies. Vienna was wonderful (again, a rabid search for pastries, distracting myself from one hunger by feeding another). Salzburg was too scenic and quaint to be believed. In Zermatt, a tiny town beneath the peak of the Matterhorn, accessible only by cog railroad, my hotel room was so cozy and delightful I took a photograph of it, wishing painfully that Thomas, or some other handsome man, were there to share it with me. Kirsch proved to be the distraction that evening.

There were the study abroad tours of England and Scotland sponsored by my department in 1994 and 1995, as well as that independent jaunt of mine to Ireland in 1994, when I tracked down my Ferrell roots and visited so many churches I began to feel Catholic. When I got to Inishmore, the largest of the Aran Islands, off the western coast of Ireland, I wanted to stay among the stone walls, huts, pubs, and blooming potato fields. The earth felt ancient there; it felt like a place where solitude and celibacy would be welcome companions. I was tired of the pursuit, tired of paying love's high price. There, I fantasized, rock and sea and wind would be sufficient company.

But of course I came back to Appalachia: part financial necessity, part attachment to family and the West Virginia hills. At home, consolation came in the form of literature, food and wine, and small professional successes. I cooked German and Scandinavian food for friends, studied books on Wicca, learned how to be polite in Greek, wrote poems. I listened to country music and stormy operas, planned my next trip overseas, attended highland festivals in my kilt, spent money on expensive Belgian beers. Perhaps at my present age—my mid-forties—if I were single, now that the hormone-fueled fires of ardor have died down a bit, such a life might be enough. Then, in my thirties, none of it was sufficient. The short time with Thomas had reminded me of what was missing. Everything else felt stale, like a series of substitutes for what I really wanted: a love relationship with a man of substance, a hope that my attachment to Appalachia and my own bad choices seemed to have sabotaged. I felt like a winter landscape waiting for crocus bloom.

A Mustache Moist with Manna

There was never a proper goodbye. There was one last meeting, one afternoon in July of 1995.

After three years without any contact with Thomas, I opened my letter box at Terrace View and recognized his irregular handwriting on an envelope. The letter explained that he and Dick had moved from New England to the DC suburbs, only a few hours from Blacksburg. Thomas still thought about me. He wanted to see me. I was still as much in love with him as ever, and so the affair rekindled.

In Falls Church, Virginia, we managed two stolen weekends in 1995, one in February, one in May, both allowed by his partner's business trips. The February weekend was an ecstatic reunion. The May weekend went badly. I was too needy, he was too elusive and withdrawn. We argued again and again, and finally I brought him to tears. For Thomas, that was too much of a threat, too much of a breach in his defenses. I left, and neither of us spoke what we feared: the relationship was far more agony than bliss, far too difficult to continue much longer.

I drove back from Falls Church alone. Instead of taking the interstate to Blacksburg, on a whim I drove up onto the Blue Ridge Parkway. I was in no hurry; there was no one waiting to meet me. As I drove, sick with grief, listening to woeful country songs on my tape deck, sunlight and cloud shadow rolled over the mountains, the new green of early May flashed by. After an hour, I pulled over to a rest stop. I strolled to the overlook and looked out over the Blue Ridge and the Shenandoah Valley, the great crests and folds, ridge after ridge, like a static sea, more convinced than ever that no lovelier landscape ever existed. In the open back of my pickup, I stretched out in the sun, head on my backpack, boots propped up on the tailgate. I stared up at the sky, adjusted myself on the uncomfortable corrugations of the truck bed, then propped my baseball cap over my eyes, and, comforted by the beauty of home, I slept.

🦋

In the summer of 1995, for a month and a half I assisted with my department's study abroad program in the British Isles. In Brighton and in Edinburgh, I composed passionate poems about Thomas, wrote him long aerograms, and looked forward to my return to the States so that I might see him again and gauge where our relationship stood. When I flew into Dulles, I stayed a few days with Cindy in her Cleveland Park apartment, which gave me time to meet with Thomas before I returned to Blacksburg. We had lunch together in Georgetown, and Thomas told me that he'd told Dick about our affair. This seemed promising: it appeared that I meant enough to Thomas for him finally to be honest about our relationship. After lunch, I coaxed him up to Cindy's apartment, gave him the silver Scottish quaich I'd bought him in Edinburgh, poured us some mead, and pulled off his clothes.

Why say "I love you" if you don't mean it, if you have no intention of backing up those words with actions? Afterward, he showered off the scent of me. At Cindy's door we shared one last hug and kiss. I walked him to the Metro. As he stepped onto the train, I remembered that morning in Framingham, three years before, his handsome face on the pillow smiling at me as I pulled the door to and left him in bed with his lover, then drove back to Blacksburg alone. Here, again, we were parting, but, unlike on that morning in Framingham, after which I was determined to have no further contact with him, this hot afternoon in DC I watched him leave believing that our connection would continue. It had proved durable despite myriads of obstacles. The next day I sat by the pool of a Georgetown townhouse where Cindy was house-sitting and wrote a poem about those lucky enough to know that the bearers of bliss would return.

"I never saw him again": most mournful of sentences. Something like John Greenleaf Whittier: "For of all sad words of tongue or pen, / The saddest are these: 'It might have been!'" That August, he sent me no birthday card, an omission that disturbed me, as desperate as I was for concrete proof that his feelings for me were still strong. When, after a few weeks of anxiety, I e-mailed him a querulous note, he responded with a vicious diatribe complaining about how petty I was, how much I'd used him, how my supposed love for him was just camouflaged and manipulative lust, how he was in the process of breaking up with Dick and had better things to do than pick out a birthday card for me.

It was as if a spitting cobra had popped out of my computer screen. Still, shocked as I was, I recognized projection when I saw it. His subsequent notes, less venomous, detailed his new lover in Atlanta, then his reconciliation with Dick, then his new enthusiasm for feng shui and his disinterest in me as anything more than a friend. We broke off contact in October of 1995, as I recall.

Almost a decade later, I try to understand him, now that I am no longer that lonely bachelor who cherished whatever sweet sparse crumbs he gave me, now that I am to some extent in his shoes, partnered but cursed with a roving eye. To have one's cake and eat it too: he admitted that that was what he wanted. That I understand. I have more than enough of the selfish child in me still. What I do not share is the apparent indifference he showed toward the effects his actions had on others.

When I think of Thomas—and I do quite often, more often than I normally care to admit—I try to wish him well, but I cannot. I wish for him what he gave me: someone beautiful, desired above all things, who trifles with him, reminds him of how sweet the world can be, then breaks his heart. I have never been able to let go of anything my memory allows me to grip: old grudges, old griefs, regrets, guilts, lost ardors and joys, like heavy souvenirs that I refuse to relinquish, afraid if I lose my grasp on my history, cumbersome as it is, I will lose my grasp on the man that history has made me become.

Poetry is just one way to hold on, to record what I feel I should not forget. Forgiveness, on the other hand, is about letting go. As easy as life might be if I could do that, I cannot. The great thing about not being a Christian, my friend Grant is wont to say, is that you don't feel compelled to forgive. I feel compelled to remember, and memory keeps passion fresh: like throwing a jar of moonshine onto a bonfire.

❦

Poem as lament, nostalgia, complaint. I have often joked that the only PhD I've ever received has been in complaining. But constantly singing dirges, however lyrically worded, gets old fast, for both bard and audience. In those years after Thomas—years wasted on celibacy and less-than-profound promiscuities, years of youth rapidly running out—it often occurred to me that my loneliness might make me heavy company, that my friends might grow very weary of consoling me, of hearing about my romantic failures and frustrated erotic longings. How fine it might be, I imagined, to give them good news for a change, to announce a long-awaited change of luck: meeting a man with substance, experiencing the miracle of mutuality.

Distance the Skeleton

He had a nickname for me those first few weeks, a term he used around his friends to describe the new guy he was dating.

"When we first met, I called you the Leather Man behind your back," he confessed one night over another rich and complex dinner.

"Leather Man?" I said disingenuously. "How did you know I was into leather?"

"Oh, please!" John said, rolling his eyes. "The shaved head? The goatee? The earring? The motorcycle boots? The rainbow flag on your backpack?"

"Ah," I said, taking another bite of chicken and asparagus rotini, then sipping the Chardonnay. "Good wine."

When people ask how we met, John always begins the story by saying, "He was my student," which folks always find interesting, since I am a teacher. We met in a Faculty Development Initiative computer class I took in June 1997. Though I am a Mac user, I had mistakenly been placed in a PC class, so I needed extra help. I can identify most trees from long yards away, but I'm not much of a technology buff. Luckily, there were several grad-student assistants. John was one of those.

During coffee breaks in Donaldson Brown, the alumni center, he and I chatted and did the sort of thing we queers do when the gaydar is going off and we want solid evidence for our suspicions. We mention significant books, people, and places. "Hey, you ever read any novels by Andrew Holleran? Do you know Dale Sewell? Any good bars you'd recommend in DC?"

We've been together ever since, with the occasional ups and downs caused, for the most part, by my problems with anger and depression and my penchant for promiscuity. His family's from New England, though he spent much of his youth in Florida, but now he's in Charleston, West Virginia, where he's found a job in his field that allows him to be relatively close to me. It's common enough in the twenty-first century, a relationship forced into long-distance mode by economic necessity (and, in our case, by my stubborn reluctance to leave my native region). The drive between Blacksburg and Charleston is only two and a half hours, so we spend most weekends and all of my academic breaks together: Thanksgiving, Christmas, spring break, and the long, sweet summer (my main reason, I sometimes think, for remaining in academia). During the week, we both work hard, and on the weekends we have friends over for big meals in either Blacksburg or Charleston. Our guests look at our overstocked liquor cabinet with amazement. "I'm a southern homosexual poet," I say. "I have to drink." They look at our collection of cookbooks and shake their heads. "Name a cuisine," I say. "Greek, British, German, Italian, Scandinavian. We've even got Transylvanian and Belgian."

It's a luxury to share a life with such a man. Fine house, small circles of friends in both towns, martinis and assorted imported cheeses from Charleston's Capitol Market, wines from Blacksburg's Vintage Cellar, complicated meals and evenings relaxing on the couch with our favorite TV show, *Charmed*, or the latest rental movie. The lonely boy I was as a WVU undergraduate, the man in despair after Thomas's departure—how could either of them, their sense of what is possible pinched and narrowed by years of romantic debacle, have ever envisioned such a future?

And if comfort makes me unappreciative, as it often does, there is always deepening middle age to shake me awake and remind me to praise the present. Lines across my brow, silver thickening in my beard, this or that joint pain at the gym. Abundance is, in the long run, always brief.

The Symmetries of Happiness

In those years between losing Thomas and finding John, I filled my days and nights as best I could. Single men and women become resourceful that way. We work hard to construct pleasures that require no one else's consent.

I watched reruns of *Dark Shadows,* a Gothic soap opera I'd loved as a child, very much relating to the vampire Barnabas Collins—his terrible secret, his outcast status, his fruitless search for love. I even had a jeweler replicate his onyx ring. What a fine escape, at the end of a day teaching freshman comp, to come home, have a beer, and watch taped episodes of *Dark Shadows.* Science fiction, with its emphasis on the future and on technology, has never much appealed to me. But fantasy and the Gothic, with their otherworldly, supernatural elements and their emphasis on the past, have always delighted me, especially when my life has felt far too prosaic or banal, an unfit receptacle for a man of my passionate capacities. After all, the appeal of fantasy is greatest when one's daily life is devoid of depth, significance, satisfaction, or interest. Ask any anomie-riddled adolescent.

Then there were the Celtic enthusiasms. My mother had descended from Cyrus McCormick, inventor of the reaper, and the McCormicks were a sept of the Scottish Clan Maclaine of Lochbuie. When I made it to Scotland on the 1994 study abroad trip, I discovered that the clan tartan, to my pleasure and relief, was good-looking rather than garish, and on a whim I bought a kilt, trying to add a little dramatic dash to my quiet English-instructor life. Upon my return to America, I began attending highland festivals and Burns Night dinners, eager to turn my back on the far-too-restrictive twentieth century and enjoy imaginative recreations of freer, more romantic times. I had, to speak archetypically, a Warrior and a Lover inside me with no outlet, no life to live but that of fantasy.

❦

A healthy marriage, I am beginning to realize, is about moderation rather than extremes. The Romantic Age: my relationship with Thomas was all extremes, with rapture one minute, sick despair the next. The Augustan Age: my relationship with John is usually calm, comfortable, and orderly. For most people, reality itself, if lived at all sanely, is about moderation, a balance of the senses and the intellect.

I am, I admit, not built well for either marriage or daily life. I grow bored easily (rather like a spoiled child). Small daily annoyances erode my patience. Only in times of crisis am I at my best, like the grandmother in Flannery O'Connor's "A Good Man Is Hard to Find," who "would of been a good woman" if there "had been somebody there to shoot her every minute of her life." I'm always on the lookout for an opportunity to fight, to emulate highland heroes and head off to battle. Warrior energy without constructive outlet, a siege mentality I cannot easily turn off. To speak figuratively, I'm always looking for something on which to sharpen my sword. Perhaps this is why I fell in love so many times with inaccessible men: I knew the triumph, if ever achieved, would be all the more delicious after such a challenge.

Now, after so many years of scarcity and disorder, I am not sure how to adapt to plenty. For decades, when I was a single gay man in a region relatively devoid of gay social opportunities, the swelling melancholy music of Puccini's *Madama Butterfly* and *Tosca* gave me greater reason to feel deeply than anything else in my frustratedly chaste life. Now I am trying to learn how to appreciate the order and symmetry of neoclassical composers. Dionysus is trying to live with Apollo. When you thrive on conflict, as many artists do, when you have a taste for tragedy, it is hard to accept (tolerate?) happiness.

A Feast Together

As incapable as I am of forgiving those who have wounded me and as much as I poison my life with my own hoarded bile, present happiness is a fine antidote.

John and I are snowed in together here in my Blacksburg apartment. The roads are far too bad for him to drive back to Charleston, so he'll simply have to miss work tomorrow. "Hooray!" we shout together, echoing the frequent celebratory refrain of the potty-mouthed kids on *South Park*.

Late afternoon, I pour us some Isle of Jura single malt and put the soundtrack to *The Return of the King* on loud while I cook. John's tapping away on his laptop at the kitchen table, and some chili is steaming on the stove. Outside, snow piles up on his Honda and the four-by-four pickup I just bought off my father. A slow storm lines the limbs of the red maple outside the kitchen window. Tonight, after dinner, after some quiet time—I'll read about Prague, where we hope to go next summer, and he'll finish his laptop work—we'll watch some taped episodes of *Dark Shadows*, then go to bed early. It will be sweet to lie in bed together, beneath the quilt he recently bought me, and listen to winter wind make the tin roof thunder. John will stroke the silver in my beard, as if it were the snow dusting spruce trees, as if age could be brushed off.

These are indeed my best days. I would be a fool not to know it. And all the sweeter, found after so much turmoil.

Not Enough

Sometimes, when John and I make the hour-and-fifteen-minute drive between Hinton and Blacksburg, as we pass through the hamlet of Ballard I will joke, "I hear tell a queer lives here." I say this because a friend of mine once corresponded via e-mail with a gay man who lived in Ballard, a lonely and closeted man looking for love on the Internet. I never met him, but I think of him when I drive past Ballard's produce stand, with every seasonal vegetable on display, a West Virginia cornucopia of garden-raised abundance. Does he ever shop there? Does he clasp crookneck squash or corn on the cob or pears and think about how easy it is to feed the body and how hard it is to feed the heart? If I had not left Hinton, if I had not met John, perhaps I would be living such a life, one in which the capacity for passion is squandered and the soul is starved.

Sometimes, tired of Blacksburg's increasingly obnoxious traffic, I dream of living in some small mountain town. Newport, Virginia, perhaps: it is close enough to Blacksburg's liberal, university-town attitudes to be liberal itself. But not Ballard, or Hinton, or most other small towns. Not if I intend to live with John and be openly gay. Not in a region so poisoned with intolerant fundamentalism. I have lived honestly for too long to return to a crippling secrecy. It would be like abandoning a kingdom and taking up residence in a pigpen.

Small towns can seem so idyllic, especially to a romantic like myself. But I try to resist that seeming, that illusion. I have heard too many stories. I know how precariously many lives are led, especially the lives of minorities, those who cannot conform or who refuse to fit in.

Summer of 1980. I've got a minimum-wage job in the recreation department at Pipestem State Park. Right now, almost workday's end, I'm waiting by the time clock with a bunch of good-ole-boy co-workers, the sort of men who would do anything for you if you were their kind, who would beat the hell out of you if you were not. I'm scruffy bearded and masculine enough to look like them, so they aren't aware of my carefully concealed monstrosity. They like me—I am, after all, a local boy—and I like them. They're not evil. Few situations are that simple. They're just ignorant when it comes to difference. How could they not be? There's a lot of heterosexuality in Summers County, but not a lot of heterogeneity.

We're passing the time, ready for the clock to hit five so we can punch out and head home. One of my co-workers starts talking contemptuously about the black security guard who works at the park. Another points out that the black man is married to a white woman. Another tells of a time when a black family moved to Pipestem. "They decided not to stay here long," he says suggestively. The other men laugh. The clock hits five, and we disperse.

Beautiful Pipestem. The woodlands, the small farms, the waterfall, the meadows full at twilight with mist and moonlight and wildflowers. A black man beaten into the mud. A black woman clutching her children and shrieking. A windshield shattered, a small house on fire, sparks swirling up into the face of summer constellations. A country night is very dark. You can so clearly see the stars.

John and I love the Capitol Market. It is our favorite part of Charleston. Inside, there are the cheese store, where we buy British and French and Spanish cheeses, and the butcher, where we buy top-quality, reasonably priced chicken breasts, bacon, and, occasionally, country-style ribs to barbeque. There are West Virginia treats like pepperoni rolls and dried ramps and wildflower honey; there is a seafood shop with top-notch oysters; there is even a bookstore. There's a bakery I usually avoid in my unceasing and generally failing attempt to reduce my love handles.

But the vegetable market, held outside in late summer, is what I love most. Farmers come to town with their garden produce, and I am ecstatic, a farmer's son no matter how many voluminous tomes I read. The peppers, the eggplants! The gorgeous tomatoes and the squash! Like the Ballard produce stand times twenty.

Today, we want to give the farmers our business and not have to drive out to Kroger. I've found some green onions and some salad. Maybe a dozen eggs—we're on the Atkins diet and we go through eggs fast. When I examine the carton, I see that the eggs are from Winesburg.

Sherwood Anderson's book *Winesburg, Ohio*, deals with small-town life. One of the stories, "Hands," I have taught in my gay and lesbian literature class. It is a story I often think of when I catch myself doing what my father does, trying to pluck every crumb from the plate. Daddy was brought up during the Depression, and so he is frugal. Every morsel must be savored, everything useful must be saved. He used to scrape the bottom of an ice-cream bowl for so long and so loudly that my mother would roll her eyes and grit her teeth. God help her, she ended up with a son just like him in this respect.

Wing Biddlebaum, the protagonist of "Hands," lived in places like Ballard. A dedicated teacher who has been wrongfully accused of trying to seduce one of his male students, he has been driven out of his small Pennsylvania town to end up eventually living as a recluse, in a state of emotional and erotic starvation, on the outskirts of Winesburg, his natural affection squelched, fearful of touching another human being. At the very end of the story, Wing finds bread crumbs on the floor, and "putting the lamp upon a low stool he began to pick up the crumbs, carrying them to his mouth one by one." The metaphor is poignant and unmistakable.

❦

It will come to us all, sooner or later. The money runs out or the love leaves. We survive with what little is left. Poverty gnarls us, yes, but it can make us humbler, more compassionate, less judgmental. It can keep us human.

When All Goes Well

Women have nurtured me all my life, starting with my mother, grandmother, and sister, and continuing down through a long line of female friends, both lesbian and straight, who have helped me through the hard times that other men—homophobes or handsome cads—have doled out to me. I laugh when some ignoramus says that gay men are gay because they don't like women. I like most women, and most women like me. In fact, women like Jessica Lange, Halle Berry, and Jane Seymour are so beautiful that they make even a hard-core queer like me understand heterosexuality. "Good God, guys!" I say to my straight buddies, when I echo their groans of lust over some particularly appealing woman. "I'm gay, I'm not blind!"

Still, it is good to get to a point in my life at which I like men equally well. For years, men intimidated me, starting with my remarkably intelligent but occasionally selfish, irascible, and difficult father. During my younger days, I long questioned whether my manhood could measure up (no pun intended) and spent years hardening myself and developing both physical and emotional strength. I feared both the intolerant straight man's response to my homosexuality and the desirable gay man's potential to break my heart or at least devastate my ego.

Now that I have settled down with John, however, I find myself in a better relationship with my father than I ever might have imagined and surrounded by good, kind, nurturing men, both straight and gay. My father sends me back to Blacksburg with home-baked bread and fresh applesauce, John surprises me with a birthday trip to Key West, Phil and Dan treat us to long talks and big dinners, Grant buys me a beautiful edition of Rimbaud, and Chris and Breck prepare us a huge brunch at their lakeside cabin before taking us out on the boat for the afternoon. Though I tend toward selfish, irascible, and difficult myself, I look to these men to learn to be less fierce and more giving. I want to be the kind of man who knows how both to box and bake bread.

❧

When we are young, if we have been raised in fairly healthy households, we do not naturally tend toward anxiety. There is that vaunted youthful sense of invulnerability, that confidence, that optimism and idealism. It takes some losses, some age, to make us realize all that could at any moment go wrong.

"What is it like when you finally have it all?" I asked my buddy Jim once. We were sipping Guinness in the Blacksburg bar called the Underground, talking a bit before he started into the dart-throwing again. Still mourning the loss of Thomas, I envied Jim greatly. He certainly seemed to have everything a straight man might want. He was young, talented, and very handsome (just my type, to my quiet frustration). His wife, Liz, who resembled a young Elizabeth Taylor, was a super cook, a great conversationalist, and a wonderful mother. Their children were sweet, good-looking, and polite. His life was so different from mine that I felt like an anthropologist studying an alien culture.

Jim smiled and took a gulp of beer. He looked at me, his black mustache moist. "Once you have it all, then all you can think about is the many ways you might lose it."

Tracks near the Hinton railroad station.

Perry Mann's farmhouse, Forest Hill, Summers County, West Virginia.

Forest Hill, Summers County, West Virginia.

Clara Mann, Jeff's mother,
Covington, Virginia, circa
1940.

Jeff and his sister Amy at Touchstone, Perry Mann's Greenbrier River camp, circa 1967.

Jeff, Clara, and Amy,
Douthat State Park,
circa 1967.

Jeff during a workout,
Willey Street, Morgantown,
West Virginia, circa 1978.

Jeff's family at his grandmother's house, Forest Hill, West Virginia, circa 1980.
Front row, left to right: Doris Roberts (aunt), Clara, Amy, Perry (father), Burt
Roberts (Doris's husband). *Back row, left to right*: Jeff, Ann Roberts (cousin).

Jeff at Brooks Falls,
Summers County,
West Virginia, circa
1991.

Clara and Jeff, Hinton, West Virginia, circa 1994.

Jeff, Amy, and Perry on the
Forest Hill farm, circa 2000.

Jeff in his kilt, Hotel Roanoke,
Roanoke, Virginia, circa 1999.

Jeff on the Forest Hill farm, circa 2002.

Jeff and Amy at her baby shower, Green Valley Bar and Grill, Summers County, West Virginia, November 2004.

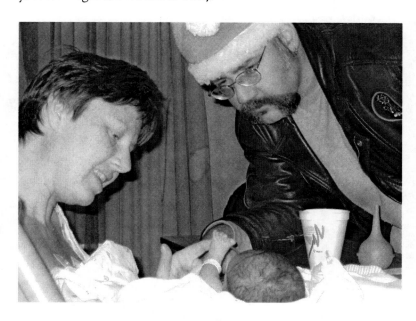

Amy, Jeff, and Amy's son Ferrell Mann, Greenbrier Valley Medical Center, Lewisburg, West Virginia, December 24, 2004.

Jeff and Cindy Burack, *Edge* book party, Ellett Valley, Montgomery County, Virginia, April 2004.

Jeff and John outside Now Voyager Books, Provincetown, Massachusetts, October 2003.

Perry Mann and Denise Giardina chatting at book party for *Edge* and *Masters of Midnight*, Visions Day Spa, Charleston, West Virginia, August 2003.

Signing *Masters of Midnight*, A Different Light Bookstore, San Francisco, California, June 2003.

Jeff toasting Sylvia Plath at the Ritz bar in Boston, Massachusetts, June 2004.

Three

Mountain Fireflies

The long drive home from lovemaking—
mountain roads, catalpa bloom, mists rising
in the first rush of rain. Ax cleft,
memory still moist with our mingling,

I stop at my aunt's for coffee. While rain shakes
the black walnut leaves, she ladles out stew,
slices coconut cream pie—recipes used for generations.
In her eyes and face and hair my grandmother lives still.

I listen for hours, tales that ended under headstones
just up the hill, the Ferrell family graveyard.
A bowl of wilted lettuce hurled at a husband's face,
the slow carcinogens of mismatched marriages.

The wife, discovering adultery, who wrote Roosevelt
and had her husband transferred across the continent.
Men staring at the gun rack, staring at the fire,
hearing the awful river ice snarl and crack.

The great-aunt, who outlived her husband
by forty years—graying alone in the Richmond
home they'd shared, leaving his shirts still neat
in the drawers, his hat and coat still hung in the hall.

Under all those gravestones, small sagas
as intense as mine. How you haunt,
how I cherish the touch we thieve
from time—their dust pulsed as such.

How the heart splits in half, dull buried
bulb with its own serendipitous seasons
rising slow and aching into petal and scent.
All as ax cleft with love as I.

I leave after the storm subsides,
looking once towards the hilltop, where

I will cease the heart-long and hunger,
the rush and cling and spin.

All about me, mountains and pastures
my ancestors worked, distant tree frogs
chirping, darker peaks of barn against
meadowed sky. And fireflies everywhere,

constellations to match the sparks
above, as if I strode the Milky Way,
pulsing with the gravitationals of stars.
Fireflies rising from the wet grass,

spiraling about the chestnut trees.
Galaxies drifting up from graves,
dispersed consanguine fires.
These fragile linkages of light.

Love Made Solid

I dream about her quite often. In the dreams, she appears looking as she always did, and I am always mildly surprised. "I thought you were dead," I say, and she shakes her head and cuts me a piece of pecan pie.

Nanny, as I called her, my father's mother, was the great transmitter of family tales. Family history as she perceived it was family history as I received it. Those stories I tell to this day.

❧

Her Aunt Nora, who has married well in the big city, returns to the Ferrell farm, loaded with bags of presents her myriad nephews and nieces receive with delight.

Finally she turns to her sister Arminta, Nanny's mother. "Min-*tie*," she pipes, "would you like to see my pus-*sy?*"

"Sister *Nora!*" Arminta gasps in Victorian shock.

From beneath her apron, Nora whips out a black-and-white-checked milk pitcher. The handle is shaped like a cat.

❧

My cousin Jimmy has gotten his high school sweetheart, Lisa, pregnant. Lisa's parents do not insist on a shotgun wedding, which is what Lisa was angling for, according to Nanny. Instead, they hide her away in a home for unwed mothers. Illegitimacy is a terrible stigma still, so Nanny hires a private detective to find Lisa before she gives birth to a bastard. A happy ending, after much anxiety. Lisa is found, she and Jimmy are married, and my sweet cousin Sarah is born without stain.

This is a cautionary tale, told to me when I hit puberty. "Now, son, I don't want to go through that again!" Nanny warns, using this tale as a pretext for explaining the birds and the bees. I promise her I will be more careful. I will be more judicious than Cousin Jimmy in the use of my "Jew-wacker," as she calls the penis.

❧

I am eating La Choy chow mein, the height of cosmopolitan food in Forest Hill, West Virginia. "Don't you want any?" I ask her.

"No, son," she says. "I just like to watch you eat. I like to listen to you hum."

"That's not humming, Nanny! I'm saying 'Yumm. MMM!'"

"Well, Carr *used* to make a fuss over my cooking, back in Norfolk. You know, son, I found out he had a woman on the side. Do you know what I did?"

I raise my eyebrows and add more soy sauce. "No, ma'am, what did you do?"

"I wrote Roosevelt and told him my husband really wanted an assignment in California, and do you know what? A few months later, Carr was reassigned, that hussy was left behind in Norfolk, and pretty soon Carr and I were having drinks at the Top of the Mark in San Francisco!"

We're driving to Alderson along the Greenbrier River when the radio announces that Elvis is dead. Surprised talk in the car commences. "Well," says Nanny, "I heard he was one of those."

I turn to her, disturbed. In just a few weeks I will be moving to Morgantown to start college; I am eager to patronize the gay bar my friends Bill and Kaye have told me about and find some good-looking man to help me lose my virginity. I can't begin to imagine how my sweet little Bible-reading grandmother would respond if she found out I loved black beards, country boys, and chest hair.

"One of those?" I ask, afraid of the answer.

"You know, son. A morphodite!"

The word is close enough to "hermaphrodite" for me to surmise what sort of person this unusual Appalachian expression refers to.

Christmas 1980. I tear open the package to discover *Secrets of Better Cooking*, which Nanny figures I need now that I have an apartment of my own in Morgantown. Inside it she's written, "When you get married give this to your wife!"

February of 1982. I am painfully enamored of Doug, a Concord College student introduced to me by lesbian friends, a short, mustached, muscular boy who necked with me down Camp Creek Road one freezing night in the back seat of a lemon-yellow Camaro. As soon as he senses that I'm interested in more than sex, he begins avoiding me.

Not an atypical response for gay men. I've joked bitterly for years, "Two gay men sleep together once, and then they refuse to speak to each other ever again. Two lesbians sleep together once, figure that means they're in love, and then move in together immediately."

Deeply despondent—time to add Doug to the long list of men who've refused me—I move into my father's empty Forest Hill farmhouse for a few days, reading Chinese poetry in translation, writing in my journal, walking the frosty farm, making fires in the Buckstove, and sharing meals with my grandmother, who lives right across the road.

Nanny cannot figure out why I am staying in the cold farmhouse by myself. She doesn't understand why I am so sad. Then, over coffee and apple pie, she says, "Son, are you in love?"

I choke back a gasp. How does she know? Old enough, I guess, to have seen these symptoms in brooding young men before.

I shake my head and return to my pie. I cannot tell her about Doug.

Today my grandmother is teaching me how to make biscuits and pie crust. I want to be able to re-create my family's home cooking for gay and lesbian friends in Morgantown, but I also realize that heritage is invaluable and can be lost if it is not carefully passed on. So, over this bleak Thanksgiving break in the mid-1980s, Nanny pulls out the rolling pin and a slew of ingredients, I pull out a pen and blank recipe cards, and we begin.

I come from a family of good country cooks, but at this age—my mid-twenties—I am still ignorant of most basic kitchen techniques. I can bench-press a decent amount of weight in the gym, identify a sourwood tree by its bark, and tell you a lot about W. B. Yeats, but I'm not sure how to fry up an egg. After several minutes of watching her bearded, bulky grandson timorously paddle pecan pie filling with a whisk, my tiny grandmother, exasperated, snatches the bowl from me and whips the mixture into a mad froth, saying, "Here, son. Harder! Like this! You have to beat it *harder!*"

By afternoon's end, I've done it. None of it as good as hers, but still, a tastily passable set of buttermilk biscuits, a pecan pie, and a pumpkin pie. The folklorists would call the events of this afternoon oral transmission. I am not yet ready to call myself an Appalachian. I am not yet willing to give up my grand dreams of a romantic, exciting life in the big city, where, I hope, many fascinating men await me, men sure to find me just as fascinating. But I do know it is important to be able to do for yourself, to be dependent on as few folks as possible. Mountain gourmand, spoiled by years of down-home cooking, I detest fast food. I am determined to re-create, wherever I might wander, something more substantial than a poem. Biscuits, sausage gravy, pecan pie: something that tastes like home.

We're driving through Bellepoint, the last year of Nanny's life, sitting in the back seat together, when a song of Cher's is featured on the radio.

"You know, I admire that woman!" Nanny says abruptly.

I am surprised. Cher is such an openly sexual creature, and my grandmother is so buttoned up and proper.

"I saw her on the TV the other day, and someone was asking her how she had the guts to wear outfits that let people see her belly button, and she said she'd wear what she damn well pleased and she didn't care what other people thought! You know, son, that's the way you ought to live. Just live your life the way you want to, and don't worry what other folks think."

San Francisco, July 2003. John and I have just attended the gay pride parade, wandering through the crowds of proud, outrageous queers—the dykes on bikes; the hot, shirtless bears; and the huge, neon-furbelowed, bespangled drag queens. A far cry from West Virginia.

Now we are in suits and ties, having martinis in the elegant bar at the Top of the Mark, a place I have wanted to see since Nanny mentioned it to me as a child. We toast my grandmother, then watch the sun set over the Golden Gate Bridge, order some paté, and grow "gently stewed," to use an H. L. Mencken phrase. We're on vacation, so, of course, a second drink is called for. Later, if the booze doesn't make us too sleepy, maybe we'll check out the Eagle, San Francisco's infamous leather bar, and the Lone Star, the bear bar.

I wonder what she would do, seeing me now, here with John, in the city of the morphodites. She would have loved him, I think. She would have been delighted, as my mother was, to know that, after so many years alone, I had him to look after me.

❧

It is hard to love folks in their flawed totality. Knowing this, with lovers, friends, and family we often omit what we can of our more controversial or disagreeable facets, trying to minimize the possibility of rejection. After Nanny died, I heard family stories from other sources, other filters, and discovered I was not the only master of omission.

Before the sweet little lady in the house at Forest Hill who baked me biscuits and cobblers was a woman I never knew. A wild 1920s flapper, hard drinking, flirtatious, a wild child from the sticks of Summers County who hit the big city of Charleston, West Virginia—this city where I type now, this city now almost a century older—and ran amuck, who matched her husband's infidelities (which she told me of) with a few adventures of her own (which she left out).

After the devoted, bespectacled, and spoiled grandson was a man she never knew. A man looking for what he could find in Morgantown's drab gay bars, making love to Paul in the flicker of the oil lamp, driving back from Framingham and the break with Thomas, numb as the icefalls along the Massachusetts turnpike. The man who likes to dance to Cher's disco mixes, wears biker jackets a lot, and is infatuated with the country music singer Tim McGraw.

I wish all those people had met. Nanny and I would have adored one another nevertheless, or, with so much complexity in common, perhaps all the more.

Firefly Porches

There were so many of them in my childhood, all of them gone now. Aunt Grace, Aunt Eula, Aunt Red, Aunt Reva, Aunt Boots, Aunt Edna, all elderly aunts of my mother's, most of them residents of Appalachia, most of them living in solid old Victorian homes in small towns. Eula, Boots, Edna, and Grace ended up in Caldwell, West Virginia, just down the mountain from Lewisburg. Aunt Grace, in particular, I grew close to, for she often baby-sat for my sister and me. She was deaf, because of a childhood illness, so I learned at a very young age to speak slowly so she could read my lips.

I remember only scattered images from those early years, visiting those aunts: heavy curtains, dark sitting rooms, hand pumps and outhouses, heavy pitchers and bowls in which I washed my face in the mornings. Summer evenings on the porch, watching fireflies rise from the lawn. Farmhouse pantries and morning glory trellises. Lemon cake, fried oysters, pecan pie with lard crust. My abortive attempts to catch the many rabbits roaming Aunt Grace's backyard. Walks along the stony creek with my father, a copperhead he killed, the fangs he showed me, prying open its mouth with a stick. Fields of Queen Anne's lace, a friendly collie, an old lady in an overheated trailer who played the autoharp. My first bus ride, between Caldwell and Covington, Virginia.

The McCormicks and the Taylors, bloodlines that gave my mother to me.

Fried Chicken and Spoon Bread

The blue urn rests on the mantelpiece. Occasionally my sister and I talk about a spring ceremony, about taking my mother back to Covington and burying her ashes where she wanted them to rest, beside her parents in the public cemetery right off I-64. But we have yet to get around to that. The earth can wait. We have barely been able to bring ourselves to sort through her clothes. Instead we cook for ourselves my mother's favorite meal—fried chicken, spoon bread, lemon cake—often on her birthday, June 26—and the urn remains where it has since February 1998, the month my mother died.

&

Covington, Virginia: where my mother grew up, where I spent the first years of my life, after interrupting her breakfast about 8:30 in the morning on August 8, 1959, the day of my birth.

Now, when I get back to Covington—very rarely, for no family is left there—I see it for what it is, a small, grimy mill town. For my first decade, however, it was the world, with its soot-gray houses and underpasses, the smell of the Westvaco paper mill, those distant, always smoking industrial chimneys. We lived at 315 Prospect Street, a stucco house in a neat neighborhood since gone shabby. I remember the persimmon tree, the mimosa, the Norway maple. I remember fear of what might hide in the closet's dark. There were Hostess cherry pies, my mother's mother's chicken-in-a-biscuit crackers, walks to the High's for lime sherbet, Halloween cat masks. My first enthusiasms: witchcraft, Batman and Robin, Tarzan, chemistry sets, rock collections. The simplicity before sexuality kicked in.

&

For most of her life, my mother was a model of passivity—like many women of her generation, those born in the 1920s—and she inculcated this passivity in me. When kids in grade school picked on me, her advice was to ignore them. "They're just trying to get a rise out of you," she'd say. "Just turn your back on them, and they'll go away." This tactic did no good, I soon discovered, though kicking them in the ass did help. It has taken me years to escape this inherited timidity and cultivate some sort of reasonable assertiveness, and to this day I have problems discerning what is appropriately assertive and what is hot-headedly, irrationally aggressive.

My mother's passivity was something that maddened me inordinately, an unreasonable reaction on my part, one that often spoiled our time together. Classic projection: I detested the passivity in her because I hated it in myself, regarding it as a handicap and a weakness, especially in a man. I was always raging against the world, she was always encouraging me to put my unseemly anger away and accept things as they were, a response that often simply redirected my rage toward her.

So, these days, when I look at a frighteningly conservative nation and ponder what it means to be a warrior in the twenty-first century, I try to remind myself that she too, with all her meek concern for propriety, could be a fighter. She often told me about a battle that had occurred before I was born, when she was working at Covington's Westvaco paper mill in the payroll department. She had trained a young man who, because of his sex, was soon promoted above her, then paid more than her. Her protests against this blatant chauvinism had eventually made a difference in company policy. This was a victory she cherished even in old age.

And I still remember weeding strawberries with her, one afternoon after we'd moved to Hinton, West Virginia, after she'd given up her job and resigned herself to life as a housewife (despite the fact that she enjoyed neither cooking nor cleaning). Someone right across the Greenbrier River started dumping trash onto the riverbank. "Slob!" she shouted. "Pig! That's illegal! I'm calling the police!" Her incensed screams drove him away posthaste. Social justice and environmental protection: these are worthy legacies.

My mother played the part of many old-fashioned southern women: she socialized me, trying to tame what was wild, smooth what was coarse, determined to raise me with immaculate manners. She was, in other words, trying to create a groomed Virginia gentleman. In fact, when we moved to West Virginia, when I was ten, she struggled to weed encroaching West Virginia pronunciations out of my speech. "'For,' not 'fer,'" she would coach. "'Our,' not 'are.'"

I was her creature for a time: an asexual, bespectacled, polite adolescent whose courteous ways delighted old ladies like my many great-aunts, a boy whose academic dedication impressed his teachers. She and my father had never had a fulfilling marriage, and my father and I were too much alike to get along with any ease, so my mother and I clung to each other. For a long while that emotional connection felt not like suffocation or vampirism but like welcome symbiosis.

But then sexual exploration kicked in during my freshman year in college—late, as with many other gay kids, who have no safe way to explore their early erotic feelings in high school—and I turned from her to a fascination with men. I returned home for Christmas break 1977 with a foul mouth, a black leather jacket, lumberjack boots, and a gray T-shirt with "MACHO" printed in big letters across the chest. It felt inevitable, that erotic imprinting. I'd grown up around small-town Appalachian images of masculinity, and so that rough-edged manhood was what I was attracted to and what, eventually, I wanted to emulate. Or at least some version of it, if you throw leavening enthusiasms for literature, botany, mythology, and man-on-man leather sex into the mix. I was tired of being a shy scholar, a mind without a body, and for a while my insecurity drove me to swaggering *über*-butch extremes.

For a time, she hated my leather jacket ("Trashy bikers wear them"), my denim overalls ("Only farmers wear them"), my WVU Forestry Club "Foresters Do It in the Woods" T-shirt ("Vulgar!") and my tank tops ("Are you going to wear *that* up town?"). She didn't know what to make of my weight lifting, my scruffy beard, and my obviously lesbian friends. She bought me elegant ties I never bothered to learn how to tie, blazers I never wore. The variety of masculinity I was cultivating was, obviously, far too uncivilized for her taste. She was completely unaware of what had catalyzed this metamorphosis from southern gentleman to apparent brute: the realization of my homosexuality and my attempt to reconcile it with images of manhood I'd absorbed from fiction and the world around me.

Then, 1978, Christmas break of my sophomore year. When I got home from West Virginia University for a few weeks' vacation, my sister (to whom I'd come out only a few weeks after I realized I was gay) warned me not to be alone with our mother. Apparently Mommy had dark suspicions and was gearing up for a Big Talk with me. My avoidance tactics were successful only so long. One afternoon, when my sister was out with friends and my father was at the office, my mother, grim faced, informed me that she had found "some literature" hidden beneath books in my room. There, in her hand, were a few queer newspapers I'd picked up at a gay bar in Columbus, Ohio.

I hesitated, sure the truth would kill her. (A standard fear among gay youth. Note to the next generation: parents are generally more resilient than that, though the nastiest among them may try to kill *you*.)

Then I admitted I was gay. She wept, of course.

"It's my fault," she wailed.

I shook my head. I probably rolled my eyes.

"It's your father's fault," she keened.

I shook my head.

"It's Jo Davison's fault," she gasped. Jo Davison, who had taken me to the Twilight Lounge, a Columbus bar where I had picked up those gay newspapers and seen my first drag show. Jo Davison, who had saved me innumerable years of confused identity.

"No, Mommy!" I snarled. "It's no one's fault."

"Will you consider going to a psychiatrist?" she asked.

"You've got to be kidding!" I'm sure I rolled my eyes then.

"I thought you'd say that," she admitted regretfully. I was too much my father's independent-minded son to consider such a thing.

The painful conversation wound down after a while, ending with an exclamation that made us both laugh. "Well," she finally said. "I hope it's a phase. I hope one day that you meet a woman who makes your penis stand up like a flagpole!"

"Well, anything's possible," I replied, "but I wouldn't hold my breath."

❦

My mother never quite gave up her dream that the right woman might change me. Her hopes were raised when I expressed aesthetic appreciation for certain women, or developed infatuations with actresses like Jane Seymour, Linda Hamilton, and Jessica Lange. Still, I was not the sort of queer who would come out and then never mention it again. I was too passionate and too honest not to voice my ardor for men, and she had little choice but to come around fast.

Pretty soon we were watching *Magnum P.I.* together and joking about my boyfriend Tom Selleck. "You ought to buy a leather cap to go with that jacket," she suggested when I came home with a new black leather jacket from Rehoboth Beach. She reveled in my stories of drag shows and the more outrageous manifestations of gay-bar life, tales that I deliberately told to remind her that there were more flamboyant versions of gay manhood than that of her semicamouflaged son. She broke the news about me to my father during an argument with him. "He was shocked out of his mind," she reported smugly. "I told him, 'See! You don't even know your own children!'"

In the autumn of 1985, while living in the DC area, I was watching *An Early Frost*, the first television movie to deal with AIDS, when the phone rang during a commercial. It was my mother, in tears. She'd been watching the movie too.

"Please be careful," she begged. "And you know, don't you, that if you ever got sick, we wouldn't turn our backs on you. We'd want you to come home."

Home. Where I would have dwindled quietly, reading many books and thinking about the many handsome men unmet. Where she would have baked me spoon bread and lemon cake, where we would have rocked on the porch together, watching the sunset over the New River, and, eventually, fireflies floating in the park.

She couldn't stand Jack. He was trashy, she firmly declared, and besides, he was twice my age. I was in love and didn't believe her, but she proved to be right. He turned out to be a callous manipulator, the first man to break my heart, a man on whom I wish a foul fate to this day.

She adored Eddie, a man with whom I had a half-hearted relationship my last year in Morgantown, West Virginia, the year before I moved to Blacksburg, Virginia, in 1989, to teach at Virginia Tech. Eddie was well dressed and considerate, the sleek sort of gentleman she'd always hoped I'd become. He bought her presents; they chattered together about topics that bored me, like furniture, clothes, and antique stores. She ended up liking Eddie a lot more than I did. They shared the same difficult and, in the end, futile agenda: trying to domesticate me.

She never met Thomas, though she was deeply disturbed that I was carrying on in secret with another man's mate. She probably wondered where my sense of ethics had gone, even though I tried to explain to her that, in the face of the Heathcliff-sized passion I felt for Thomas, morality was a picayune, ineffectual, ultimately irrelevant thing.

She loved John, my present partner, whom I'd met the summer before she died. One of our last conversations, the day before her death, was about John. She knew he would be graduating from Virginia Tech soon, and she was afraid employment opportunities would lure him away and I would be alone again, as I had been for most of my adult life. "I don't know what's going to happen," I admitted.

I didn't know. But I wish I could have seen the future and consoled her, promised her that I had found a man who would stay with me. A man who would hold me hard the next day, after the hospital-bed vigil was done, a man who takes care of me still.

My mother smoked for most of her life—Pall Malls. I often worried about her health and begged her to stop an obnoxious habit that might take her from me earlier than necessary. As a child, I had even dripped water onto her smoldering cigarettes when she wasn't looking, trying very deliberately to slow down the erosion of her lungs. As an adult, I tried, on some deep, unspoken level, to prepare myself for her loss.

Perhaps my irascible distance in her last years, a distance I now regret with painful frequency, was an unconscious attempt of mine to detach myself from a love I sensed I would soon lose, a separation designed to spare myself pain. If so, it was a cowardly act. In her last years, her health waned—breathing problems, a minor stroke, a weakening heart—and slowly the passivity and stasis she had always displayed began to define her completely. She seemed incapable of creating a life for herself, apart from her husband and children—the bane of many women of her generation, I suspect. More and more, she clung to me—like a person sliding down a steep mountain slope who seizes whatever vegetation is at hand. She resented, perhaps envied, the many aspects of my life apart from her—the travels, the friends, the short-lived affairs—anything, in other words, that kept me from coming home as often as possible. Her love for me often felt like interference, like a threat to my emotional autonomy. It was terrifying to be so depended on, as if I were the only source of her happiness. I felt guilty living a life apart from her, leaving her to dwindle in that small mountain town she had never learned to like, much less love.

❦

February, the month people die. I was still in bed with John in Blacksburg when the phone rang. One of the reasons I've remained in my native region of Appalachia is to be easily on hand if my family needs me, and that morning such determination paid off, because I was in Hinton after only an hour and fifteen minutes.

My mother had caught a cold that, because of her fragile condition, had dangerously escalated. She didn't want to go to the hospital, but there was little choice. The sun came out as she was carried up to the ambulance. I filled out hospital forms, I conferred with doctors, I even caught myself cruising a big-shouldered, beefy-chested, goateed intern and wondering if any extremity would prove sufficient to blind me to an attractive man's charms.

Those years of smoking and inactivity approaching agoraphobia had made her too weak to fight off pneumonia and a stroke. She faded with the afternoon, soon slipping into unconsciousness. My father arrived, emotionless, matter-of-fact, and stayed only long enough to sign the necessary papers. A kind nurse put on soothing music. I sent my sister home, firmly convinced, as I have always been, that I am stronger than anyone I know—and therefore the only one capable of keeping a deathbed vigil. Gritting my teeth, I fought back tears and for the most part succeeded, having been brought up to avoid unseemly displays of public emotion. I held her hand and swabbed her lips with a moist Q-tip. I watched the electronic display of heartbeat slow and stop.

I packed up her few things—dentures, eyeglasses—thanked the nurses for their professionalism and compassion, and left. As I waited in the hospital parking lot for my sister to pick me up, the moon rose over the mountains and a doe moved through the woods. Comforting omens, for a Wiccan like me.

That night, I dreamed that I saw my mother in the grassy park before our house. The leaves on the trees were the new gold green of spring. She was smiling. She kicked up her heels like a child, as if delighting in her escape from encumbrance.

❦

My many years of loving the wrong men have ended, perhaps for good, and my life with John is as comfortable and respectable as my mother would ever have hoped. I wish she could have lived to see not only the early chapters of my life—struggle, loneliness, constant strife—but these middle years as well. John and I share a fine home in Charleston, West Virginia, a split-level with cherry paneling, tasteful furniture that he picked out and that she would approve of, a great view over the city, a library of cookbooks, a cozy den and fireplace, and a king-sized bed. I have a tenure-track job at Virginia Tech at last, and have had several books published, all successes in which my mother would have rejoiced.

John has taken over the challenging task of domesticating me, I'm sure she would be relieved to know. *Someone needs to do it,* I imagine she'd say. There she was in his eyes, deeply disapproving, when I revealed my first tattoo, a barbed-wire armband. When, gripped these days by a minor midlife crisis, I whine for a motorcycle—a Honda Shadow would be perfect—and John shakes his head, my mother is there too, pursing her lips and quoting death statistics. She is also there in less discordant times, when I have the flu and John makes me hot toddies and homemade chicken and dumplings, when I have a new poem or manuscript accepted and John buys me champagne.

❦

I get back to Hinton occasionally, to see my father and sister. When I return, there is the blue urn on the mantelpiece. In it rest not only my mother's ashes but a stone I pulled from Castle Moy on the Isle of Mull, the seat of the Scottish clan to which my mother's family, the McCormicks, belong. When I leave, there is no one in the back bedroom window waving to me as I drive away, as she always used to do. Strange to be an Appalachian, to teach Appalachian studies and discuss the legendary closeness of mountain families, yet to have so little family left.

Regrets linger. One I have discussed above: the distance I wedged between us in her last years, for reasons that I, to this day, do not entirely understand. Unhappy myself, in that long loneliness before John, I could not with any grace deal with her unhappiness. She was a woman whose life had been filled with disappointments, a woman who had dreamed of love and ended up in a long and loveless marriage, a woman who had dreamed of big cities and glamorous travel and spent most of her life in small, conservative, uneventful towns in Appalachia. I am sure that my emotional withdrawal only added to that litany of disappointments. It must have felt to her like abandonment, bitter as the withdrawal my father had managed inside their marriage. Even now I find the memory of her deep discontent intolerable.

The other regret involves, of course, the major way I failed to live up to her hopes: my homosexuality. Before I became a sexual being, the pallid intellectual I was disappointed her. I believe she had hoped for a regular boy, a hardy sort who played football. She once told me that the only calluses I'd ever get would be from turning the pages of a book, one of those casually cruel things that a parent says and immediately forgets saying but that linger forever in the child's mind. Always concerned with what other people thought, she was probably worried about what the neighbors said in private about the bespectacled, pudgy bookworm poring over volumes on the occult. Surely I was not masculine enough, ordinary enough to satisfy her. Always, mixed with her love, was mild disapproval.

In this respect, my father's relative indifference to both me and to public opinion felt like a blessing: he didn't much care what I was or what I did. My mother, on the other hand, was concerned with everything about me: what I wore, what I read, where I went, whom I befriended.

When I became a sexual being, there was the manliness she'd always wanted, but in a form too rough to be respectable. More importantly, this finally achieved manliness was queer, the largest disappointment of all. What good was it finally having a masculine son if he pursued men? What good was it having a son with weight-lifting calluses if the muscles he'd developed were for gay-bar display?

In this context, some lines from Sylvia Plath's *Three Women* have always haunted me. In fact, one evening, after too much bourbon, I read the relevant section to my mother. A woman who has just given birth to a son muses about his future:

> I do not will him to be exceptional.
> It is the exception that interests the devil.
> It is the exception that climbs the sorrowful hill
> Or sits in the desert and hurts his mother's heart.

Instead, she wills him to be common, to love her as she loves him.

All my life I have been the exception, a fact that often caused my mother much chagrin. The intellectual among the provincials, the bookworm among the athletes, the pagan among the Christians, the poet among the illiterate, the hillbilly among the city folk, the queer among the straights, the leather jacket among the suits. As I age, I am more and more thankful not to be average or ordinary. I relish my peculiarities and contradictions, the odd amalgams that compose me. Open nonconformity feels more and more like a necessary political act in the America of the early twenty-first century, with hate crimes on the rise and gay and lesbian civil rights contested hotly on all sides. Honesty, however risky, is what we owe the next generation.

These days I sometimes wonder how she would feel about the balance I've achieved among my many selves—the artist-scholar, the Wiccan, the Appalachian, the musician, the traveler, the bearded leather man, and all my other odd identities. I bake a linzer torte for John, write a poem, shave my head, read some Icelandic literature, plan a trip to Prague. I cast the circle for a May Day ritual, play my dulcimer, wash my four-wheel-drive pickup truck, head down to the gym to take more boxing lessons or work on my preacher curls. I think she would approve of everything except the tattoos.

Only for my mother's sake do I sometimes wish that I had been "normal." "Common," to use Plath's word. It is a moot point, since so little of our lives feels chosen. She is gone, and I am what I am. Still, she might have been happier with an average son, one who enjoyed phys ed, majored in business, brought home to her a daughter-in-law and grandchildren. Average, I might not have hurt her heart quite so much.

What occurs to me only now is this trenchant irony: what hurt my mother's heart the most was not my exceptional nature, but what was common in me. What is more common than a man too unsure of his own strength to be compassionate? I cannot forgive myself for my irritable lack of compassion in her last years.

One thing is comforting to remember, in the midst of the guilt welter that some children feel after a parent's death. By the end of her life she clearly was not ashamed of me. In fact, she admitted to anyone who would listen that her son was gay. She, the woman who had disapproved so often of so much of what I was, would brook no disapproval, no unkind words aimed at her son or at any other gays or lesbians. On this topic, she would rise from illness, depression, and old age, and she would fight. She railed at local fundamentalists, conservative politicians, and open homophobes with nearly as much vigor as I do. In the midst of ambivalence—and what parent-child relationship is not fraught with that?—there is this one clear thing: her love for me gave her the courage to fight a battle she never chose.

I want to think of that when I finally relinquish my mother's blue urn to Virginia's earth, when my sister and I plant daffodils and lilies of the valley around the grave plaque. Afterward, we will drive back to West Virginia. We will sit out on the deck overlooking the Greenbrier River, sip some bourbon, talk quietly in the gathering dusk. Then we will cook up a big southern meal of fried chicken and spoon bread. Perhaps we will even collaborate on a lemon cake.

Her Kitchen's Square of Sunlight

Family versus "family." A basic conflict for the gay or lesbian Appalachian. "Blood is thicker than water," my mother always said, and when I was recovering from yet another handsome man's indifference, I used to agree with her. Much has been said about the Appalachian attachment to family.

But in the gay community, biological family is often something to break away from. Some of us do it to avoid rejection; afraid to tell the truth about ourselves, we create a protective distance. Some of us are forced to leave our families behind in order to escape their sometimes violent reactions to our sexuality.

So we speak of "Family" as a substitute: the gay community in general. "Is he Family?" we ask. "Ah, nice to be among Family," we sigh, entering a gay bar after a day spent with straight people. More specifically, when we say "Family," we have in mind the gay and lesbian friends to whom we give the energy and devotion usually reserved for parents and siblings.

So many gays and lesbians have to relinquish one family for another. Often the choice is made for them by the screams of a father or the cold shoulder of a sister.

Blessed among queers, those of us with supportive relatives, those of us who do not have to choose.

My junior year in high school. I'm walking down the crowded hall on my way to typing class when I pass one of my name-calling nemeses near the auditorium. He's a good-looking kid, with a muscular, hairy physique—a man's body, not a boy's—which I can't help but admire. I hate him nevertheless. Because he's short (and, I must note with vindictive amusement, often wearing clunky shoes with big heels in an attempt to look taller), he insults me only when he's traveling with his pack of friends. As he is today. "Faggot!" he growls as I walk by.

Coached by my mother to ignore insults rather than avenge them, I stick my nose up in the air, walk faster, and pretend not to have heard the hated word or the snickers that follow it. It's then that my little sister appears out of the stream of students hurrying to their next classes. It's her first year in junior high, her first year at this school. She stands before my accuser, pretends to laugh with him for a few seconds till he's off his guard, then suddenly shoves her middle fingers in his face and shouts, "Fuck you! FUCK you!"

Dwarf-boy's face cracks like thin farm-pond ice beneath a lobbed stone. My sister is bigger than he is. His jackal horde nervously disperses—no one's going to hit a girl, for God's sake, and this one's enraged—and within seconds his big heels are clopping hurriedly down the hall.

❦

Amy and I have so much in common. Our values are almost identical, the predictable mountain attitudes that Loyal Jones summarizes so neatly in his essay "Appalachian Values." We love these mountains, we are attached to family, we do for ourselves, we both love to cook down-home southern food, we regard mainstream America, urban America, dubiously. We hate the same things: bad manners, incompetent child rearing, conservatives, spendthrifts, bigots. Common hatreds and common loves—what else makes a relationship? And, when it comes to our choice of spouses, the majority would not approve. Her husband is black. My husband is male.

Before John and I met, during those many years full of bitterness, complaint, and regret, coming home was a wonderful break from my loneliness. My sister is a caregiver par excellence, and spending time with her, enjoying her meals and her conversation, seeing in her the same sort of country caring that my grandmother embodied, began to make of Hinton and its surrounding hills not a prison but a shelter.

Dispersed Consanguine Fires

Being gay and being Appalachian sometimes feel to me like mutually exclusive states of identity. So many gay men and lesbians, faced with rural intolerance, relocate to the big city, where urban gay communities provide them with both friends and lovers.

God knows I love to visit cities and luxuriate in queer culture. In DC, there's Lambda Rising, the gay and lesbian bookstore, and the Green Lantern's shirtless night, when I can peel off my shirt, drink free beer, and rub up against all sorts of sweaty, furry guys—bear buddies of mine who relish city life. In San Francisco, there's the swarm of leather daddies and dykes along the Castro, and, a little further up the California coast, there's the Russian River region, with its gay western bar and the guest ranch Fife's. In gay meccas like Provincetown and Key West, there are gay bed and breakfasts, bookstores, restaurants, and bars. My vacations with John often center around these places.

But what if you don't want to live in cities? What if you were brought up with such traditional Appalachian values as attachment to family and to place? What if you detest the urban annoyances of noise, traffic, overpopulation? What if you'd rather hear bobwhites than disco beats? What if you prefer oak trees to skyscrapers?

That summer of 1991, meeting Thomas as often as I could, contemplating his imminent departure, I asked myself whether I would be willing to follow him to Boston, if he were single, if he asked me to, if our circumstances were different. The only good thing I could see about his relationship with Dick was that I would not have to make such a choice. I loved mountains, I loved men. The two passions seemed inimical to each other. Choosing one, I would have to turn my back on the other. In this situation, at least, the choice had already been made, and not by me. It had been made by Thomas. Despite his attachment to me, an attachment whose depth I was never able to gauge, he had made it clear from the beginning that his life with Dick was his first priority, and that his plans for the future all involved urban settings.

So I found myself in the abject position of so many who have loved those whose first loyalty lies elsewhere. I cursed Thomas, I cursed Dick, I cursed my own perverse and foolish heart. Trying to set my suffering in a larger context was one of the few consolations I could find. Often, as I drove back and forth between Blacksburg—where Thomas and I shared our furtive afternoons together—and Hinton—where I still lived at the time—I would stop at my Aunt Doris's farmhouse for a visit.

My Aunt Doris lived her last years alone, having dispensed with a series of lackluster husbands. She kept up her farm in Forest Hill, West Virginia, raising geese and chickens, spaghetti squash and corn, Johnny-jump-ups and hollyhocks. I admired her humor and her independence. I visited her often, sometimes bringing frozen lobster tails as a treat. She'd brew coffee, spoon out green beans, serve slices of fresh-baked bread and coconut cream pie, my favorite dessert. We'd talk for hours, about this and that, before settling in to watch old movies.

I never told her I was gay; I never mentioned Thomas or any of the many other men I'd loved over the years, every one of them a mistake. But the stories she told about our family put my loneliness and my pain, my Celtic melancholy, in perspective. "Honey, we Ferrells don't become alcoholics, we marry 'em," she'd joke, referring to her own bad choices, ones she'd grandly survived. Those tales reminded me that I was not the first or the last to suffer, to yearn for what could not be had, not the first to be crippled by overblown hopes and perfervid intensities. The sort of connection I sought to share with Thomas had been sought by my ancestors, sometimes successfully, sometimes not. Knowing that my story was only one of a long line helped me survive.

My Aunt Doris died suddenly, in August 1994, in Bowling Green, Kentucky, where she had moved only a year or so after I had shared beef stew and coconut pie in her kitchen, listening to those family stories that made my own tormented little saga with Thomas make more sense. For years she had boasted about escaping the effects of smoking, but then she came down with a fast-moving, mysterious illness. One week she was bowling, the next week she was dead. Only after her death did the lab reports confirm that the cancer had started in the lungs.

I was one of her pallbearers. She was buried with her bowling ball. She died not knowing I was gay. She was a devout Baptist, and I had always feared her reaction. I read "Mountain Fireflies" at her funeral.

Now, when I go to the Ferrell family cemetery with John, we visit Aunt Doris's grave. Her headstone is decorated with a quilt pattern and a spool of thread, reminding me of the bear-claw quilt she once made for me, the same quilt John and I sleep beneath when we visit Hinton in chilly weather. How I wish she had met him. I brush leaves off the graves, look out over the surrounding ring of mountains, tell John a few more of my family stories, and feel a great acquiescent peace. I am eager neither to age nor to die, but if mortality must be—and of course it must—knowing I will one day join kin there is a great comfort. It seems appropriate, like the last couplet of a sonnet.

How the Wilderness Feeds Us

Great-aunt Sadie spent her life single in Summers County, the classic mountain spinster, with her gray hair wrapped tightly in a bun. Did she have failed love affairs with men in her youth? Was she a repressed lesbian, whose natural inclinations were crushed by mountain religion?

I have no idea. She was a devout churchgoer, so if she was ever assailed by unseemly attachments to women, she must have guiltily buried those feelings early on. As prim and stern as she was, I can't conceive of her as a sexual being, and I can't imagine her understanding my homosexuality, had she ever known of it.

I only know that, during the difficult times of my life—the death of kin, the departure of love—I have admired Aunt Sadie's ability to live on next to nothing in that small house in Hilldale. Poverty, whether physical or emotional, can crush, but in her case it bred strength, determination, and resourcefulness. She gathered creecy greens and wild strawberries, helped my father and me tap maple trees, banked her coal fires, and stitched her quilts. She eschewed the modern and the superfluous. To her, nothing seemed necessary but her religion, her garden, and her few remaining relatives.

Aunt Sadie endured a long, hard-working, solitary life, as she endured her last illness in the hospital bed my father moved into the living room of our Hinton house. I was in the ninth grade and had never witnessed dying, so I avoided that room. Then one day I got home from school to find my mother in tears and the bed in the living room gone. Sadie is buried in the Pisgah churchyard in Hilldale, beneath an oak tree, not too far from the farm where she planted and harvested year after year, not far from the rocky soil where she gathered creecy greens.

I wish she could know the man I've become. I no longer avoid painful duties. I am the one in the family who keeps vigils by deathbeds. Someone has to. Now I am strong enough.

Loss and the Daily Biscuit

Perhaps it would have been easier to turn my back on the Appalachian region if my father weren't such a native son himself. Ever since I was a reluctant child, he has been inculcating mountain values and skills in me. As soon as he can, he leaves his law office and heads outdoors. In spring he's planting potatoes and corn; in the summer he's harvesting bushels of vegetables (name it, he's grown it); in the autumn he's chopping wood, mulching the gardens with fallen leaves, bringing home turnips and kale; and in the winter he's reading book after book, listening to classical music much too loud, cooking up great meals based on the garden produce he's canned, and poring over seed catalogs, dreaming of next year's harvest.

Facing some of my greatest losses, I have thought of my forebears, making do, living on only what they grew themselves, and I know I have had an easy life and have endured very little. When I savor my father's fresh buttermilk biscuits, I know that love, for men, is a thing often expressed obliquely. And when I walk the Forest Hill farm with my father—its great oaks, its weedy pond, its dilapidated barn and red cedar groves—I know this is a landscape I can never leave, because I am too much his son to live anywhere else.

When I was still in grade school, my father handed me a copy of Emerson's essay "Self-Reliance." He was an intellectual, a liberal, and a nonconformist, and he knew I was cut from the same cloth, so giving me Emerson was his way of arming me against the hostilities of the conventional, the right wing, the intolerant: enemies he knew we would share.

What a great gift, along with all the other literature he introduced me to over the years. Self-reliance equals independence equals a small bit of power. When, at age fifteen, I realized I was gay, Emerson's ideas were to come in very handy. There are few existences more emotionally isolated than that of a queer kid growing up in a small mountain town, and self-reliance is a healthy response to this isolation, which persists throughout Appalachia and other primarily rural parts of the world.

My father learned the many skills necessary to keep up a small farm from his paternal grandfather, Allen Mann, who, in the early twentieth century, lived on Tunnel Hill, the mountain through which the legendary John Henry dug a railroad tunnel. I have inherited some of those skills— I can, for instance, chop wood in a semieffective, half-assed way that improves with practice—but some skills I never learned well enough to lose: how to split shingles with a froe, how to harrow a field.

But, as Carrie Kline has illustrated so movingly in her wonderful readers'-theater piece *Revelations: Appalachian Resiliency in Gay, Lesbian, Bisexual, and Transgendered People*, queers in Appalachia have benefited greatly from mountain independence. It's painfully true that we're not accepted in many of our communities, and many of us must live lives of secrecy, but the same Appalachia that flays us with its strict moral codes also teaches us how to survive what pariahs sometimes suffer. Self-reliance, toughness, resilience become enviable sources of dignity and strength.

Closet Dark

Some darknesses we choose, some we are forced to bear. With every honest word I write or speak that is read or heard, I insure the impossibility of my own retreat into omission and secrecy. Going back to the closet— that is no longer a choice.

Certainly anyone who reads the *Charleston Gazette* with any frequency knows what breed of man I am. My father, Perry Mann, takes pleasure in baiting and harassing conservatives in his frequent letters to the editor and op-ed essays in that newspaper. A few years back, in response to a fundamentalist minister's tirade against homosexuals, my father published the following.

Hatemonger Preachers Could Inspire Violence

My son is gay. Further, he is not normal. He never has been, nor ever will be.

I knew that he was not normal the day he was born. There was something about him that was different and the difference became more obvious as the years passed. When he was in the fourth or fifth grade I went to a parent-teacher meeting. His teacher took me aside and revealed to me in hushed tones that my son had an unusually high IQ. She seemed in awe of it.

My son showed no interest in what normal children showed an interest in. Early he became interested in witchcraft. He wanted every book there was in print on the subject and I bought him a library of them. But witchcraft eventually took a back seat to nature and poetry.

He graduated as valedictorian of his high school class. He had an A in every subject he took from the first grade to the 12th, except for a B in physical education. He just couldn't cut the jock curriculum.

He graduated from college Phi Beta Kappa with majors in forestry and English. He eventually got a master's degree in English and then a teaching position in a college. He has been teaching English in college ever since. And he has been writing poetry with a degree of success measured by the number of publications that have printed his works and by the praises he has received from fellow poets. And if diligence and singlemindedness will bring fame and fortune to a poet, he will have fame and fortune someday, for no poet ever worked at his trade with greater daily dedication than my son does.

But I am told almost daily by very righteous people that my son is abnormal, a sinner and an abomination in the eyes of God, and that he will certainly go to hell and burn for eternity.

The latest to tell me so is the Rev. Randy Wilson, pastor of a Baptist church near Belle. He not only tells me that my son is doomed to hell but that my son is not appreciated in this society and not welcome in the state of West Virginia by him and I presume by his Baptist congregation.

I take no offense at the preacher's defamation of my son, for I have heard it all before from the same kind of hatemongers as preacher Wilson. I consider the source. He and his kind know that spewing hate from a pulpit with rabid passion to a receptive audience makes for a moving Sunday sermon. They need to unload their hatred, for it is a burden to carry around day and night.

I take no offense, but I am disturbed by the virulence of the preacher's diatribe and his ignorance of the effect such bigotry has upon other bigots. He says homosexuals do not have to fear Bible-believing people because no Bible-believer is going to mug them or burn their homes. Bible-believers may not do the deed but they can inspire others to do it.

Preachers preach because they believe they can influence people to act in a manner they consider godly. For Wilson to preach that my son is a sinner, wicked, hell-bound and not welcome in this state is on the verge of exhorting the faithful to action and causing the mad-dog righteous to act upon his words with violence.

Preacher Wilson must not have read much farther in the Bible than Leviticus. If he had, he would have read Christ's sermons and noticed—if his mind could escape from its capsule of hate for a moment—that what Christ preached and what Wilson preaches could not possibly have come from the same God.

Can anyone who has studied Christ's words visualize Jesus with burning eyes and twisted mouth vilifying a group of people as fit only to be ostracized and exiled? Christ admonished that one should judge not, and that one should be aware of the beam in his own eye before noticing the speck in the eye of his neighbor.

Preacher Wilson categorizes gays with pedophiles. He exhibits ignorance in doing so. He sneers at the suggestion that gays are born gay. He exhibits ignorance in doing so—and also a lack of insight as to why he is who he is. He bases his hate upon the Holy Bible. He manifests a woeful ignorance of that book.

He insists that gays are evil and abnormal, thereby manifesting a mind that many people would judge to be subnormal.

In general, his concepts and allegations exhibit a mind beset with simplisms and biases, all of which are conjured up to create the high of hate, and to express it in raucous righteousness to the amens of his fellow homophobes.

I am heterosexual, an orientation that I did not choose. It just happened that at puberty I found girls attractive, rather than boys. God knows that if I had had a choice, I would have chosen to be heterosexual, for who would choose, if he had a choice, to be homosexual only to suffer the taunts and jeers and the threats and thumps of straights as well as discrimination in every aspect of life? Only a fool would.

And I dare say that anyone who believes that gays choose to be gay is a bit of a fool. And for one to say that their cries "are nothing more than a smoke screen to cover them, while they weasel their way into our society as normal people" manifests a mind pervaded with misconceptions and given to reckless rhetoric.

Homosexuals through the ages have contributed greatly in every category of human endeavor. I for one appreciate them and welcome them to this state, the Rev. Randy Wilson and the Baptists to the contrary notwithstanding.

St. Paul had a thing about gays, but he also said that of faith, hope, and charity, the latter is the greatest virtue. I add that to hate the sin and love the sinner is as much a riddle to me as the Trinity. By broadcasting the riddle, it appears that religious gay-bashers want to have the high of hate and the respectability of righteousness too. It's hard to do.

There is strength in openness. When an anonymous homophobe recently sent around to all presidents of Virginia Tech alumni chapters a nasty e-mail note complaining about my website and the gay-themed publications listed there, I felt mildly threatened, but I had nothing to hide. Had I been tentative about my identity and only partially open about my sexuality, such an assault might have driven me back into the closet, but, as it was, hiding was not an option. There was my website, available in cyberspace for anyone to view. Ignoring such ignorance or fighting back were more appealing alternatives.

As it was, Lucinda Roy, the chair of my department, answered the attack on me with an e-mail note to those same alumni chapters. Her response was so eloquent and so poignant—she referred to her own experience of prejudice as a black woman—that the reptile was never heard from again. Reading her defense of me (a little moist eyed, I must admit) I thought of Lee Maynard's *Screaming with the Cannibals*, in which Jesse, a mountain boy, and Jason, a black man, sit together on a South Carolina beach, minorities taking comfort in one another's company.

The darknesses we do not choose, what can be done about that? For every woman and man, sooner or later the black birds come home to roost. Now I have much of what I've always wanted—a wonderful spouse, a quiet apartment, a good job, friendly colleagues, a slew of friends, a slowly waxing professional reputation. Now I, as my friend Jim put it over beer and darts ten years ago, wait to see when the erosion might begin, how I might begin to lose, piece by piece, the treasures gained through luck, persistence, and the gods' goodwill.

Four

Pietà

(for Allen Schindler)

1

I found them this May in Lucerne and Bern—
marble pietàs, stark white, as if
in that vaulted Gothic darkness
frost had sealed each brow, each fold
of cloak, each loincloth, each limb.
Lilies and roses flanked them,
and the banked rows of votive candles—
I bent over the guttering heat of
all that hope, all that wax-dwindling memory.
The great arch of the marble chest,
stilled in death, stilled in art,
son sprawled at her feet, or limp
over her knee, his mouth grotesquely,
realistically agape, *agape* fled,
no clutching warmth of hers
ever again borrowed or lent.

2

Driving home after two weeks in Europe,
along the windy Appalachian back roads
I love, I avoid a tortoise plodding
midasphalt. Wanting to stop and move it
into safer woods, in a hurry I guiltily
drive on. What sort of breed
would laughingly veer over it, enjoy
the sick crunch, all of evolution's
care in chiseling that carapace
crushed by steel radials, a blob
left to flatten further and reek amidst
the blooming vetch and multiflora rose.

3

In the bear pits of Bern
I saw civilization's germ.
Made safe only by yards of concrete

pit wall and the simple law of gravity,
I watched the bears gambol,
sit on haunches to catch between
their fangs the tourist-lobbed carrot nubs.
"Oh so cute," someone squealed.
How many feet above us all would they tower,
how long would those teeth and claws
made remote by modernity continue
to rend a corpse? Against that,
the first fires flared, the first walls
were heaped, the first flints chipped.
Stones piled on stones—
the Cyclopean sheers of Mycenae,
the hearths and crossbows of Windsor,
Vienna's high baroque—all culture
allowed by surplus allowed by safety.
Barricades built against bear maws,
and against this viciousness with little fur,
with dull teeth and only fingernails,
rending with fewer reasons than any bear.
A human face, from less harmful brethren
indistinguishable.

4

Trying to track down Jack the Ripper,
the detectives, desperate, pried free
the retinas of a murdered prostitute
to discern what final image rested there.
Christ's last sight, perhaps,
the burning rooftops of Jerusalem,
the tufted helmet of the man
who'd so precisely held the nails.
Cirrus scudding over what would be Israel,
the fine dark fur storming over his chest
and streaming down his belly, leading
the little sweat a high wind allowed, the blood
a spear inspired, to soak the slipping loincloth.
Better than porcelain stained with urine,
scuffed toilet tissue, the grit built up on

a public bathroom floor, the mud lining
a temple-crushing boot. Or your own blood
filming your sight, fading quickly
into darkness, as, stained with volcanic ash,
the most vivid of sunsets subside.

5

Reading the newspaper, each of us
attends his mother on that plane to Japan.
There will be no pietà, the artistic
dignity of a pose worth marble.
There is too little left to hold.
His body burst from hers, yet
all she can recognize are tattoos.
Perhaps for a few lucky seconds
in so short an adulthood, tattoos
once wet beneath the lips of a lover,
tattoos tasted, then traced with
drowsy reverence by sap-sticky fingers.
Why write on the pulsing ephemera of skin?
Like this ink on paper so easily torn,
so easily burnt. With Mary,
we hold that body close,
then lower it with great care,
an ossuary of glass.

Witness

Larry Gibson is a witness. He is speaking tonight about mountaintop removal in this crowded room in Torgerson Hall, here at Virginia Tech. He describes the ways the coal companies steal land, drive people away, rip up the landscape and leave what few residents are left to deal with the terrible environmental consequences. I want to shout "Testify, brother," for, though I do not hail from a coal-mining region of Appalachia, my father brought me up to revere nature, and my Wiccan spirituality locates the divine in the natural world. Mountaintop removal—destruction of the beauty God has made—is, to me, far more of a blasphemy than desecrating a cross—disrespect shown to a man-made symbol of God.

Soon enough, however, when members of the audience begin to respond to Gibson, I want to crawl under my chair. I was raised to hate confrontation, and now the arguments are crashing out. Miners raise their voices, talk about the importance of jobs. A colleague of mine— normally a quiet, polite sort—loses his temper and accuses a speaker of disrespect. So many injustices in this region, so few simple answers. Easy for me to hate mountaintop removal when I am comfortably employed as a teacher far from the coalfields, here in Blacksburg, where I get "a case of the ass," as my sister Amy would put it, if Kroger is out of Greek olives or arugula. I know I am "spiled," to use the Appalachian pronunciation.

My sister's husband is black, a fact my mother never quite reconciled herself to. My mother was born in the early 1920s in Virginia; some generational quirks can never be surmounted. She had enough trouble with me being gay. Talk about dual crosses to bear, in a small West Virginia town, if you cared what people thought—and my mother most certainly did. "Nigger-lovers and queers," Amy and I used to joke. Add to that my father's passionately liberal opinions, his hatred of Republicans, consumerism, fundamentalists, and the NRA, and you have the most colorfully freakish family in Summers County. Only my mother, bless her, was normal.

My brother-in-law, Michael, is from a large family in Talcott, West Virginia, where the legendary black folk hero John Henry is said to have lived and died. It has been interesting, for a man like me, who's spent most of his life around other white folks, to get to know Michael's mother and siblings, to see how similar black and white Appalachian cultures are. The use of language is similar, with a few exceptions; the food is the same, with a few exceptions. (I would like to try fried chitterlings, though my sister tells me the boiled variety smells nasty.) God knows I can make a significant path through Mama Joyce's green beans, barbeque, rolls, sweet potatoes, and coconut cake. "Soul food" is pretty much what we whites in Summers County grew up on too.

As a gay man, I have always felt a kinship with other oppressed groups. But what struck me when a couple of Hinton's petty-minded racist cops roughed up Michael one evening down by the Greenbrier River is how easy most gay folks have it.

I figured out pretty early on, once I realized I was gay, that camouflage was a good way to avoid attack. It did little good in Hinton, where I already had a reputation as a quiet, polite bookworm (read: fag), and where I buddied around with the discernibly butch-femme couple Bill and Kaye. But when I got to Morgantown, I cut off my long hippie hair, grew as much of a beard as I could manage, took phys ed classes in self-defense, and began lifting weights. I bought my first leather jacket, inspired by the role models Patricia Nell Warren's novels had given me: Vidal Stump, the motorcycling, priest-seducing hero of *The Fancy Dancer,* and Danny Blackburn, the leather man/sadomasochist/cop in *The Beauty Queen.* In other words, I was not only emulating men I found appealing, I was learning to blend into the straight world so I wouldn't get another split lip like the one I received from a gay-basher in high school.

But of course most black folks can't pass. Some of us white queers, we can hide our sexuality in potentially dangerous situations. Blacks can't hide their race.

So I was particularly moved, reading Lee Maynard's *Screaming with the Cannibals,* when Jesse, the hillbilly hero from Wayne County, West Virginia, after escaping his hometown—an urge I recognized—is befriended by a black community in South Carolina. Sitting on a beach reserved for blacks with his new friend Jason, who gently explains to him the ugly facts of racism in the 1950s South, Jesse muses, "I felt comfortable there with Brother Jason, two guys who had absolutely nothing in common, just sitting on a beach. But maybe we did. Maybe we were two guys who never had anything, maybe never would have anything, maybe didn't know where we belonged, maybe didn't give a shit about all the things that everybody else gave a shit about. Maybe there wasn't any place for us" (194). There it is, the warm fellowship of exiles, those witnesses to injustice. The tight bonds created within oppressed subcultures are a support and a blessing that members of the spoiled mainstream must live without. I think I would prefer to endure prejudice and hardship than live unthreatened and unharassed but without that misfit warmth.

Streaming Fire

One autumn in the late 1990s I attended the Goldenrod Writers Conference in Morgantown. While there, I sat in on a workshop led by the state poet laureate, Irene McKinney. She suggested an interesting exercise: to examine the body of your poems, determine what tone you tend to take, then write a poem in a completely different tone. I go for somber, lyrical, romantic, and elegiac in my poetry, but in my daily speech I'm often funny, bitchy, sarcastic, caustic, and irreverent. I'm often pissed off about something: small things like barking dogs, car stereos, and bad manners; big things like homophobic fundamentalists, idiotic politicians, environmental shortsightedness.

From my father, I inherited a nasty, scatological, cruel sense of humor: anger sublimated into dark laughter. He's always joking about using a sword to run through an obnoxious dog or delegate, always suggesting that Preacher So-and-So needs an acid enema. He's also always trying new vegetables in his garden, and one summer, without knowing what lava he was dealing with, he grew habanero peppers.

Habaneros are almost useless. One of them is sufficient to heat up a huge pot of chili. They are the hottest peppers in the world. Still, since Daddy grew them, he and my sister canned them—like dealing with the vegetable equivalent of plutonium. I love a challenge, I'm proud of my ability to produce and to endure intensity, so there I sit every now and then, cutting a slice of canned habanero into tiny, tiny shards and eating them with pieces of pizza or on top of brown beans. I sweat, I curse, I wipe my brow and grin. I am a Leo. My patron element is fire.

❧

My partner, John, must be a little disconcerted when we watch sci-fi movies together. Often, a sort of vicarious battle frenzy overtakes me, the same excitement I felt reading superhero comic books as a child. When a character in such films blasts his foes with some preternatural power like telekinesis, storm summoning, or fire throwing, I'm ecstatic, on the edge of the couch, shouting, "God! Goddamn! I wish I could do that!" John shakes his head. He probably shudders, imagining the smoldering corpses my hair-trigger temper might leave behind.

I know that urge, that yearning for destructive might. I know that hot dream of escape: from the restrictions of law and order, from the human body's limitations and weaknesses. What queer kid who's survived those painful years in high school doesn't thrill to Stephen King's *Carrie*, in which a much-abused misfit is humiliated at her prom and uses her tele-kinetic powers to slaughter most of her classmates? "Do it, Carrie," some part of me shouts. "Do it for all of us!"

Sometimes I want to live in twelfth-century Scotland, or somewhere similar—perhaps J. R. R. Tolkien's Middle Earth—where my rage could be given sufficient outlet, where solutions to conflict would be frequently simple and brutal. Give me a dirk, I think, and five minutes with Jerry Falwell, Pat Robertson, or Fred Phelps, that execrable swine whose followers displayed placards scrawled with "Fag Matt in Hell" when Matthew Shepard was killed by gay-bashers back in 1998.

Thus, big-screen sword-and-sorcery movies, like sci-fi movies, get me "het up," as we Appalachians would say. I gasp and tense, clench and shake my fists, suppressing, for the sake of my fellow moviegoers, many a manic laugh and rapturous shout. I want to be part of the heroism, part of the battle. What are movie monsters and necromancers to me if not pious queer-hating Christians, or executives whose greed dooms another mountaintop?

Not only do I have a terrible crush on scruffy-bearded Viggo Mortensen, who plays Aragorn in the recent *Lord of the Rings* films, I sometimes wear a copy of Aragorn's ring and have a replica of his ranger sword hanging on a wall in my Blacksburg apartment. On some level, I'm doing the same thing I did in college, imitating Patricia Nell Warren's black-leather heroes, or, closer to home, certain macho mountain buddies I admired in my forestry classes. Trying to incorporate what I admire. Why do I, who once, as a teenager, was such a lover of Merlin and other wizards, find myself, at age forty-five, wearing around my neck the Viking rune for Tyr: warrior?

❦

Where do I get this rage? For the last week or so of Christmas break I have been reading Robert Moore and Douglas Gillette's book of Jungian psychology *The Warrior Within: Accessing the Knight in the Male Psyche*, trying to figure out the source of my fiery temper and some constructive outlet for my anger. It's a not-uncommon quest for men. As a high school intellectual, I had a hard time developing any strong sense of my own maleness, especially when I discovered my homosexuality and began having to deal with the effeminate stereotypes connected with men who love men. As a college student, I self-consciously cultivated my manhood, emulating the strength I saw in literary role models. Now, in my middle age, as a gay man who relishes body hair, beards, black leather, and boots—the signifiers of the masculine in himself and in others—now I find myself trapped in my own testosterone, so to speak, trying to learn anger management with all the other hotheads and raving bastards. Rage erodes my relationships, with my partner, with friends, with family. It's something I've got to learn to harness, because I know it cannot truly be dismissed. Writing, lifting weights, beating the punching bag—they help, but they are not enough.

❦

His name was Shorty Bennett. I wouldn't recognize him now if he sat on my lap, and I didn't know who he was then, that night that he punched me. I was, ironically, walking a female friend home, as we southern gentlemen tend to do. Sally and I were in front of what is now the Summers County Public Library when he and his thug friends drove by and shouted, "Queer!" I gestured at them dismissively and kept walking.

The car stopped in the middle of the street. Though I have no memory of how he looked, for the sake of this telling, let's describe him as a lumplike slob. (Writing as release, writing as revenge.) The driver, a lumplike slob of twice my bulk, stepped out of the car, strode over, and accused me of giving him the finger. That succinct gesture that says "Fuck you!"—that's something I would do now, angry as I am, looking for an excuse to pummel someone deserving, some loathsome homophobe, rapist, racist, some swine picketing an abortion clinic. God, I would enjoy that. (See? I have a problem.) But then I was meek, with no more sense of how to defend myself than a rabbit has. Well, rabbits run, at least, and I was too proud, too afraid of hating my own cowardice, to run.

"I didn't give you the finger," I said simply. Then his fist slammed into my mouth.

Now there's a real man, punching a kid like that. The sort of man who aims for the weak, travels in packs with others of his ilk, and gives the whole male sex a bad reputation.

I don't remember much. To this day I have a partial memory block. My glasses must have gone flying. Sally must have stepped back against the wall in horror. I can't recall whether he punched me a second time. I think so. I do recall being shocked beyond words, amazed that anything like this could happen in downtown Hinton, right on the main street. The young often have a limited sense of what's possible, and that's often a blessing.

Then Terry Bailey, a guy I hardly knew, a big muscular boy, older brother of my sister's friend Frances, appeared around the corner and took up my defense, for no reason other than a sense of justice, fair play, and compassion. I remember nothing else, other than that I apparently took Sally home (polite even when stunned), making my way home through the back alleys, for fear of running across the lumplike slob again, and woke the next morning with a swollen lip so huge I was too humiliated to attend my grandmother's Thanksgiving dinner that afternoon. I tried to convince myself that I was too pure of mind to do other than turn the other cheek, but the truth of it was that I had no idea how to be hard, how to be tough, how to fight back.

Terry, I never thanked you. I have spent my life trying, with only moderate success, to be what you were that night. I have toughened myself for the next brawl, physical or otherwise. I want to be able to defend myself, yes, but it is time to put this streaming fire I have inside to use fighting for others. As you did that night thirty years ago.

In *The Warrior Within*, Robert Moore and Douglas Gillette claim that "[t]he Warrior's aggressive potentials must be dedicated to some power beyond his own, or he becomes purely destructive, creating unnecessary conflict instead of serving and protecting the human community" (154).

Somewhere, in some small town in West Virginia, a gay teenager is contemplating suicide, a lesbian college student has been thrown out of her parents' home. I know these things go on. I have heard enough stories, from friends, from students, whose families were not as understanding as mine. A woman hangs herself in her barn. A man is dragged to death behind a pickup truck.

For gay people, simply being open and out is equivalent to taking up a sword. Honest speech is the edge I hone. May it help destroy what needs destroying.

Ephemera

January 2004, Huntington, West Virginia. John and I are gleefully feasting on a Swedish smorgasbord, at a benefit for a rape crisis center. I love Scandinavian cuisine. Close to my beloved German food in its weight and depth of flavors, and such a treat not to have to cook it myself, here in a state where good ethnic restaurants are few and far between. I am almost through my second precariously heaped plate of meatballs, pickled herring, potato salad, deviled eggs, and creamed cabbage when my hostess introduces me to Justen, a young man from Boone County. Shy, intelligent, handsome, Justen is leaving West Virginia within a few days, heading to Los Angeles to start an internship.

He's leaving in the nick of time, our hostess explains, because he was openly gay in his home county and now feels that he cannot return there safely. Justen was punched, insulted, and threatened by fellow high school students. He suffered from depression and contemplated suicide. Finally he fled Boone County and was informally adopted by a sympathetic gay couple in Huntington, where he continued his education in a more liberal environment.

As I sit there, sipping my glogg and gorging on rice pudding, I try to imagine being openly gay in my home county of Summers, now or back in the 1970s, during my high school years. I think about all the omissions I managed, the lies I told, the many ways I shielded my true self from sight, and I shake my head. All my big butch passions for swords and Scottish dirks and leather jackets, the courage I've cultivated for twenty-five years, and this kid, a head shorter than me, this kid's bravery puts me to shame.

When, at evening's end, I hug him goodbye (gay men do a lot more hugging than straight guys), I'm hugging some gutsier version of the boy I was at his age, the kid hot to get out of West Virginia and make a home somewhere less hostile. Will he miss brown beans and cornbread, the local dialect? Will he miss the blooming redbud and sarvisberry in the spring, as I did? I hope not. I hope he loves Los Angeles. I hope he meets a slew of available men, finds a wide-ranging circle of friends, and I hope he stays.

Forgive me the fantasy. I assure you that, outside the purlieus of my dreams, I am relatively harmless. But daily life is rarely intense enough for my taste, especially now that middle age thickens about me. Reality so often seems inadequate and restrictive, so seldom accommodates free expressions of my lust and my rage. If one were allowed to choose one's ideal afterlife, paradise for me might be composed of two things. One, ravishing all the many, many men I have yearned for in life but never possessed. Two, wreaking my revenge on all those who have crossed me and those I care for.

Because this revenge is fantasy, the laws of probability are entirely on my side. None of my opponents has a gun, which, in real life, would end my rampage within a minute. And, because it is fantasy, I feel no ambivalence, no guilt, no fear of consequences, just pleasure. I stride through Boone County swinging the Aragorn sword—a good ten pounds' worth—and one by one off come the heads of all those who have mocked or harassed Justen. Rather than perform the unseemly manic dance of decapitated chickens, these bodies simply slump to the ground. It's like a cornfield after the stalks have been cut and shocked: the stumps of the recently truncated. I wipe the rich blood off my blade, hum a murder ballad, then head over to the next county in search of another just harvest.

In June 1991, while Dick worked late at a nearby bookstore, Thomas and I took a walk together. We ended up in a patch of woods on the outskirts of Blacksburg. Once we were in those woods, out of the public eye, I became affectionate. He was very handsome, our hours together were always short, and touching him was a rarity and a rapture I could never get enough of. So, as soon as the leafy shadows surrounded us, I stroked his hair and then draped my arm around his shoulders.

When Thomas resisted this simple affection, afraid we might be seen, it suddenly struck me how different heterosexual and homosexual relationships are in this regard. For gay men and lesbians, public displays of affection might invite homophobic violence. Single for most of my adult life, I had almost forgotten this fact. Now, beside a man so desirable I found it difficult to keep my hands off him, I was reminded of how dangerous it is for two men to touch, especially in rural and small-town settings, where everyone knows everyone's business and there are no sheltering gay communities or liberal urban neighborhoods in which same-sex couples might feel safe. As attached as I am to the mountains of Appalachia, for once I wished Thomas and I were in DC's Dupont Circle or on San Francisco's Castro Street.

Walking with Thomas, suddenly paranoid, I couldn't help but think of Hester Prynne in Nathaniel Hawthorne's novel *The Scarlet Letter*. She enters the forest to meet Dimmesdale, her former lover; and the wilderness, as scholars have often pointed out, is emblematic of lives beyond convention, beyond society's pale (both literally and figura-tively). So in the forest, illicit lovers, out of sight of puritanical eyes, might be together. But what if, in those woods, the lovers are found by hostile witnesses? The danger might be even greater than in small-town streets. As strong as both Thomas and I were—vain gym regulars—I knew how easily we might be surrounded, how easily blades pierce skin, stones shatter skulls. I thought of being discovered in this fairly isolated place by gay-bashers and wondered what sort of violence might flare up, who might be injured, who might or might not survive. I remembered Sarge, a black lesbian I knew from my hometown, who got involved with the wrong people, a drug-dealing crowd. Year after year, that familiar face on the post office bulletin board. Then, nearly a decade after her disappearance, those sad bones found in the town dump.

I am addicted to women warriors. Perhaps it is because I was nurtured when I came out by a coterie of lesbians. I howl with delight when movie heroines kick assorted piggish asses. One of the things I like about neopaganism and its eclectic mythologies of god and goddess is how many different ways of being a man and being a woman those myths depict. Dionysus, the gentle god of wine. Athena, the implacable goddess of war.

Ideal, I think, is a combination of the fierce and the tender, which is what I've always aspired to. It's an amalgam I've found more in women than in men, who are not brought up to deal with tenderness gracefully. Certainly, had my butch buddy Bill appeared on the street that night I got my face punched, she would have tried to feed Shorty Bennett his own testicles, and, with her karate background, she may well have succeeded.

I do know that I would have been outnumbered and left bloodied that night in the early 1980s, outside Morgantown's Double Decker. A gaggle of four roughnecks was hovering outside the gay bar when I approached the door with several lesbian friends.

"You don't want to go in there," the largest growled, apparently unable to recognize queers when he saw them. "It's a gay bar."

"We know," I growled back, looking him in the eyes, clenching my fists, straightening my shoulders, and pushing out my gym-inflated chest. I had as many friends as he had. I was tired of scuttling in the shadows. Every shouted or mumbled insult, every "Queer!" or "Fag!" I had endured in high school, came back to me. I was tired of being meek, and besides, I had backup.

He took a few steps back. I took a few steps back. We circled each other, snarling threats and scorn—the behavior of two men who are too proud to back down but who don't really want to fight, two men who want to save both their reputations and their noses. Finally, after enough display to salvage our egos, he and his buddies dispersed with gestures of contempt, and my crew of sapphists and I entered the bar.

A few weeks later, drinking beers with the same group of women, I curiously quizzed them. Would they have backed me up if a fight had broken out? "Hell, no," they all said, "we'd have run." All of them except Cindy. "I'd have fought," she said quietly. The woman who was constantly harassed by classmates her senior year in Bobtown, Pennsylvania, that year she was dating the female basketball star on the sly. The woman who was threatened by her lover's psychotic mother. The woman given no end of grief by her well-meaning but fundamentalist family. Oh, yes, she'd have fought. I can't imagine a better comrade in arms.

The students in my gay and lesbian literature class, in the autumn of 1998, how confident they were that benighted prejudice was a relic of the past. They simply couldn't relate to the stories of oppression and secrecy we read. Most of them were from northern Virginia, the DC suburbs, where tolerant attitudes seem much more prevalent than in Appalachia. They found the stories I told them of my own younger days interesting, perhaps pathetic, but certainly not immediate. It is easy to forget what the rest of the world can be like when you are sheltered in a liberal university town.

Then, midsemester, there were the faces of my students in the candlelight, before Burruss Hall, that October night, the vigil for Matthew Shepard. How stunned they must have been, as if some reptilian anachronism from the past had appeared to disembowel the enlightened present. As I stood on the podium and read a poem to the crowd—a poem about Thomas, about stepping out of a DC gay bar together and looking cautiously around for gay-bashers, on a street known for recent attacks—I was not stunned by the fact of Shepard's murder. My friends and I had had a few close calls ourselves. I had heard too many local stories, I had read too many newspaper accounts of hate crimes. Allen Schindler, for instance, an American gay sailor found murdered in a public restroom in Japan, mutilated so badly his mother could identify his corpse only by his tattoos. What surprised me about the death of Matthew Shepard was how young and how small he was. I could have lifted him with one arm, I think. I am often a cauldron of hatred, much to my partner's and kin's dismay, but what killed Shepard was beyond any hate I have ever felt. Two big guys ganging up on a boy that small. There is a cowardice there I simply cannot comprehend.

Justen, I am too much of a country boy to believe that Los Angeles is safe. Be careful. Stick to the gay neighborhoods after dark. Remember how fragile we are. Eat lots of Mexican cuisine for me, and good California seafood. Check out the bars and the beaches, and drop us an e-mail including the most outrageous details. If you ever get back to these mountains, let me know, and John and I will have you up for dinner. Name the cuisine and cocktails of your choice. If you come home missing West Virginia food, you don't have to go back to Boone County to get it. Fuck Boone County, or at least those in Boone County who were cruel to you. Come here, and we'll feed you brown beans and cornbread, chowchow, wilted lettuce, new peas and potatoes, ramps and creecy greens, biscuits and gravy. You name it. All you have to do in return is tell us about the sexiest leather guys in LA and the most garish drag queens. We're starved for misfit color in these here provinces.

Five

Aeolian

In this mode fog is gathering
C minor in walnut dells.

The leaves drop, yellow moisture,
cast off so discourteously.

Amidst New England asters, another
wayfaring stranger shoulders

his delicate dulcimer, strings
loosened so as not to snap

in cold or loneliness. He falls
in love only with all he knows

is leaving soon. The odd thatch
of black hair on the outer flank

of the hand, the small smooth spot on
a chest otherwise pelted: details only

the reverent retain. Aeolian autumn
is stunning the pastures, finger picking

the first threat of frost, a fragile dew.
A man in the city stands on a rooftop

in a Sargasso of rooftops; a soldier
in the Sahara reads letters from

West Virginia and squints with salt.
Wayfarers insulate themselves as best

they can, in denim, in leather, in
another generation's scraps, the pieced

salvation of quilts, the memories
of commensal body heat. They move

in minor keys towards hearths
whose fuel they themselves

with straining backs in dream
provide, towards broad beds alone,

towards mulled cider and soup beans,
a family graveyard, a mountain tune.

Finding Solace

Melancholy runs in the Irish side of my family, and sometimes when I'm sad, I tune my dulcimer to the Aeolian, a minor mode, and play "Poor Wayfaring Stranger" or "Pretty Polly." They are autumnal songs. They remind me of loss and human fragility, love and hate, my own extremes: concepts I dwell on just enough to make sure I don't take for granted the time I have left. My partner John's handsome face and quiet kindness, the tangled fragrance of virgin's bower, the young man with the pale skin, hairy chest, and honey-blond ponytail lifting weights beside me in the gym, the hawk's flight over Lost River—I want to admire what I can while I can. Beauty both highlights our mortality and gives it solace.

Once, years ago, John woke me from a dream. I had just heard a beautiful but terribly sad song, I explained, wiping tears from my eyes, one that captured all the tragedy of Ireland's history. No doubt that song was in the Aeolian mode, like the history of Appalachia and the history of homosexuals.

So much of those histories—the lives of my mountain ancestors and my queer forebears—is about isolation and siege, hardscrabble survival, both physical and emotional, and bald-faced injustices that insult that concept of individual freedom on which America is based. Both worlds have had their martyrs: Sid Hatfield, Matthew Shepard. Homophobia, like racism, is perhaps no more virulent in Appalachia than it is elsewhere, but nevertheless fear of it keeps me from kissing my lover in public. Fear of it makes me lift weights, slam the punching bag, and wheedle a friend into giving me martial arts lessons. What I can't help but see sometimes, reading about gay-bashing in Charleston or murder in Fairmont, is a pietà, a parent clutching a crucified child, or, less conventionally, one man cradling his wounded lover in his arms. In the face of pain, personal or public, we twist this way and that in a mad search for solace.

I brood. John claims it's worrywart blood I get from my family. If there's some grudge that needs toting, some pessimism that needs preaching, I'm the man to do it. I'm worried about a gay kid I hardly know who's recently moved to LA. I'm wishing crashing cascades of ill fortune on several of my partner's co-workers, silly cows who have not treated him with the proper appreciation and respect. I'm concerned about a friend's suspicious pap smear. I wonder how Laura and Kaye are doing, two college friends who've recently lost their elderly fathers. I wonder how much longer John will be able to endure my erratic moods, frequent pouts, promiscuous urges, and free-floating hostility.

When I worry about Justen, a small-town boy wandering about Los Angeles; when I remember Matthew Shepard, Allen Schindler, or Mark Bingham, the gay man on that 9/11 plane that crashed in Pennsylvania, and think about how no one was there to save them; when I need reminding of how much warmth and generosity human beings are capable of, I have dinner with family, friends, or mountain-bred colleagues like Alice Kinder, with whom I can be entirely myself. Something about sharing home-cooked food (and, I must admit, a few drinks) lifts the spirit. Perhaps eating and drinking remind us of the natural optimism of the flesh and the delights of the daily, so often overshadowed by larger anxieties. It is a challenge, focusing on the present, trying not to muse pointlessly on the past or the future as our brains are wont to do. Fried pork chops and buttermilk biscuits help.

I've taught Appalachian Folk Culture twice now at Virginia Tech, and that course always reminds me of why I stay in this region. Folklore creates a kind of comforting group identity, a strong, unspoken bond. It is hard to leave folks who talk like you, eat like you, sing the same songs as you, predict the weather the same way you do. Many of my students already know the ballad "Barbara Allen." They know that black wooly-worms mean a bad winter. They know that snow banks that refuse to melt mean that more snow's likely to come. A few even know what wilted lettuce is, or a gee-haw-whimmy-diddle, or a sugar-water spile.

I lay that groundwork first, that commonality. When, later, I talk about other sorts of subcultures' folklore, when I casually come out and describe what a bear is (a hairy, bearded, husky gay man), or what "Woof!" means (what one bear attracted to another says, i.e., "Woof! Man, you're hot!"), there is probably some cognitive dissonance—"This guy is queer?"—but soon enough I'm back to talking about hulling black walnuts when I was a kid, or how I helped my father chop wood or make maple syrup, and their heads are nodding again. Their view of what's possible in the world widens a little bit, I'm hoping, to take me in, anomaly that I am.

Even in Heaven We Cannot Forget

"*Who would have thought the afterlife* would / look so much like Ohio?" says one of my favorite poets, Maggie Anderson, in her poem "Beyond Even This." Our daily world sags with moderation, for the most part. Life after death, in contrast, is depicted as either agony or rapture. The afterlife is always limned in extremes.

John and I are visiting my best friend, Cindy, in Columbus, Ohio, this October, 1999. Cindy long ago reluctantly left that DC apartment where Thomas and I spent two emotionally complicated nights together over a decade ago. She taught in Florida for a while, hated its conservative politics—a state where it is illegal for gay men or lesbians to adopt children—then found another teaching position in Ohio. She and I are more alike than any two people I know—separated at birth, we joke—and it is sweet to spend time with her, strolling the streets of German Village, a hopelessly quaint neighborhood of brick streets, beautiful homes, and orange-red maple trees. Also good to escape to a real city for a change, to see recognizably queer people on the street and give the beefy, bearded ones, the bears, the leather-clad ones, flirtatious glances, a roving eye that John amusedly tolerates. Odd circle of narcissism: for so many years modeling myself on the kind of men I found attractive, now often attracted to men who look like me.

I am a typical Appalachian mutt in terms of ethnic origins: English, German, Scots, and Irish. For the most part, the Scots and Irish roots of my family are the ones I have researched: trips to Longford, Ireland, and Scotland's Isle of Mull. But more and more the German blood is on my mind. Only a few summers ago, I discovered that our branch of the Mann family came from the Palatinate region of Germany, which perhaps explains my taste for the sweet Rhine wines I used to share with Thomas during our afternoon rendezvous in a friend's borrowed A-frame down Cedar Run Road. Certainly my German background helps explain the enthusiasm with which I tuck into Teutonic fare wherever I find it, whether on a European vacation with John or here in Columbus, at one of the two German restaurants I love to visit. Anyone with any knowledge of food history can see in such mountain fare as wilted lettuce and pickled beets the influence of German settlers. Like the Pennsylvania Dutch, we Appalachians love our sweets and sours.

🦋

Even amidst abundance we cannot forget starvation. Sometimes I begin to take my comfortable life with John for granted. Easy for an intensity addict, and besides, it is human nature to be restless, to yearn for the new, to be perpetually dissatisfied, to ache wistfully, amidst however rich a present, for whatever in the past has been irrevocably lost. But then I remind myself of how lonely I was in Thomas's aftermath, and then the opportunity to be walking with my partner and my best friend through German Village on the way to several steins of beer, some sausages and sauerkraut, seems like a blessing beyond description.

🦋

Strange to be an Appalachian, to love the landscape and the small towns, the winding, ice-edged streams, the burning maples of October, the shocked cornfields, the home cooking and the folk songs, yet to know how unwelcome I might be in so many of those small towns and homes.

Sometimes, for a change of pace, John and I allow ourselves a fattening breakfast at Cracker Barrel, the restaurant that specializes in downhome southern food. Until recently, I had joined a boycott of the chain, because the company discriminated against gays and lesbians. "Cracker Barrel, we hardly knew ye!" I'd keen longingly as we drove past the one in Christiansburg, Virginia, or the one in Beckley, West Virginia. I've boycotted many businesses because word was that they were homophobic or owned by individuals who were somehow politically offensive, but avoiding Cracker Barrel was the only boycott that proved painful. They serve versions of all the food I grew up on: turnip greens, chicken and dumplings, country-fried steak, biscuits, blackberry cobbler. As an Appalachian, I felt right at home with such a menu. As a gay man, I felt thoroughly unwelcome.

Now that Cracker Barrel has reversed its objectionable policies, I happily patronize them again, but, as John and I tuck into big plates of sausage gravy and biscuits, I look around the room at all the straight couples and families and vacillate between a cozy feeling of belonging and an uneasy sense of dissociation. "It makes no sense, this nagging anomie," I think, sipping coffee and shoveling in another rich mouthful. "I'm as much a country boy as any of these guys."

Sometimes, on the way to Charleston, I drive down Cabin Creek, ostensibly to avoid paying that last turnpike toll, but really just to get closer to the woodland and the creek. I drive past homes, some cozy, some ramshackle, and try to imagine the people inside. They say "cain't" like me, they love brown beans and cornbread like me, they probably like Kathy Mattea and Tim McGraw, chop wood for their stoves, and root for the WVU Mountaineers. Sometime I think, "These are my people," and I feel a rush of warmth for folks I've never met. Sometimes I think, passing this or that Church of Christ, "If they knew who I really was, some of these folks would want to stone me." It takes so little to make me shift from a sense of belonging to a sense of exile, and then into rampant paranoia.

❦

Strange to be a man of German descent, walking what's left of the concentration camp of Buchenwald. A Globus tour, summer 1991. I have come to Europe both to get a glimpse of one of the countries my bloodlines come from, and also to get away from the affair with Thomas for a couple of weeks. I am hopelessly in love with him, and already I have some sense of how bereft I will be when he leaves town at summer's end.

I love Germany: its architecture, its food, its music, the literature its sons and daughters have created. But Buchenwald's crematorium gives my romantic despair over Thomas and my childlike enthusiasm over things Teutonic a much-needed perspective. Before the ovens, heaps of flowers have been placed on the floor, in memory of those who died here. A Jewish couple I've gotten to know begins to weep. I stare into the ovens' immaculate, ash-free interiors and think of Thomas's body, my body, ending there. How long would we have survived camp life? Two men, one short, one tall, both with pink triangles stitched on the breasts of their uniforms. How long would my love have lasted under such duress? Would

I have sneaked him some of my hoarded food, or selfishly refused to share with him bits of moldy bread or watery soup, as he—in 1991 Virginia, not 1944 Germany—so generous with his beautiful body, so often refused to share his heart?

❧

Appalachia's log cabins and Germany's half-timbered homes. Ramps and sauerkraut, fried apple pies and cherry strudel. *The Dollmaker* and *The Sorrows of Young Werther.* I love the cultures that gave birth to my blood, but I have too much of a knowledge of history, too much self-knowledge, to feel entirely at home anywhere. Even in America I don't feel entirely at home, when the president of the nation takes a public stand against gay marriage, when the Religious Right gains more and more political power. There is something to be said for a ghetto: Jewish ghetto in Prague, Appalachian ghetto in Cincinnati, gay ghetto in San Francisco. In a ghetto, what began as fate begins to feel like choice.

Regional Oddities

Nonconformists are made uneasy by homogeneity. When John and I visited Park City, Utah, last summer, we loved the dramatic landscape and found the people quite friendly, but there was something weird about being the only discernibly gay people around. No black folks either, a fact explained to me by a friend upon my return to Virginia: blacks were, up until 1978, not allowed to become full members of the Mormon Church.

Something about the ubiquity of commercial American culture disturbs me. It's vaguely horrifying to find a McDonald's wherever you go. When I drive east from Blacksburg and pass through the mess of fast-food joints, malls, and car dealerships along 460, some part of my soul shudders. I keep thinking of a scene from Denise Giardina's novel *The Unquiet Earth,* in which the host of a program about Christmas in Appalachia asks the television audience, "Why do people want to stay here? How will we bring them into the mainstream of American life?" My favorite character, Dillon Freeman, an irascible miner and union organizer, a warrior if there ever was one, shouts, "Mainstream of American life! Sonofabitch! Coal companies been shoving the goddamn mainstream of American life down our throats since my papaw's day."

Testify, brother. Testify!

A stranger knocked on my door a few days ago, during my winter break, those weeks in between semesters, time I was spending in Charleston with John. When I looked at her quizzically, a little annoyed to have my writing time interrupted, she handed me a note that explained that she was the unemployed mother of two children, and she was trying to raise money by selling sassafras root for tea. Normally I send solicitors packing, whether in person or on the phone. But the curmudgeon in me hesitated.

"Where'd you get it?" I asked.

"My brother dug it in Greenbrier County," she said. "Do you know how to brew it?"

"Oh, hell, yes!" I replied. "Haven't had sassafras tea for years. Glad to get it."

Low on cash, I gave her a five-dollar bill. She looked at it as if I'd given her too much. "Don't you want more for that?" she asked, holding out her collection of little bags full of root chips.

I shook my head, she smiled weakly, and off she went to the house across the street.

I had forgotten that little bag in the refrigerator. This afternoon I will brew up some tea, sweeten it, and sip it while I write. I'll leave a little for John to sample when he gets home. I like to remind the transplanted New Englander that there are many good reasons—starting but not ending with me—to live in West Virginia.

❦

My sister once took a photograph of my father displaying one of his homegrown cabbages. It fills his lap, and he's smiling proudly, fit descendant of those German farmers who began our family bloodline. I can see him already wondering what uses he will put it to. Not sauerkraut, as his grandparents used to make. That tradition no longer continues in my family, which I regret, for I like few things more than sausages and braised sauerkraut. Fried cabbage, perhaps. Or cabbage rolls, which my grandmother learned how to make in 1930s Charleston, when she befriended a Hungarian immigrant. Maybe chowchow, something most Americans have never heard of, the sweet and sour home-canned relish so many mountaineers like atop their brown beans.

Whatever he did with that monstrous cabbage, you can be sure none of it went to waste. If there's anything we Appalachians revile, it's waste. We use, as Daddy has often put it, "every part of a pig except the squeal."

❦

The fall of 2003, one of my favorite Appalachian Folk Culture students told me a story I'll never forget. A cousin of hers from the Midwest came to visit, the surly adolescent sort. When the grandmother of the house sat the family down to fried apples, grits, scrambled eggs, and sausage gravy with biscuits, the cousin snorted, "This is a hillbilly breakfast! I want to go to McDonald's." I don't know how that particular family responded, but I know what I would have said. The little bastard is welcome to his Egg McMuffin. I'd be more than glad to clean an ingrate's plate.

So Many Gifts

If that ungrateful brat thought that sausage gravy and biscuits were hillbilly cuisine, I'd like to see the look on his face if his grandmother ever handed him a bowl of turnip greens.

My city friends tell me that, in DC, you can find greens only in the grocery stores located in black neighborhoods. I have a sudden, painful vision of expatriate queer Appalachians in their tiny, overpriced apartments yearning for good biscuits, barbeque, and bowls of greens. Beet greens, collard greens, mustard greens, turnip greens, kale. My father has grown them all. They are the sort of rough, filling, healthy, cheap food that poor people eat. True folk food.

I want to read poems about greens. I've read Lucille Clifton's poem "Cutting Greens" and Rita Dove's poem "Sunday Greens." So why don't white folks write about greens? Way past time for a queer white boy to compose such a paean.

Mama Joyce's kitchen is always hot. The woodstove seems to be going in all sorts of weather. She's quilted a lot since she retired, my sister's mother-in-law, and she's always cooking for her very large extended family. She lives up Pie Holler. The road sign says "Pie Hollow," but no one pronounces the word that way. Her hospitality is unmatched. If, come Christmas, I get a few of her rolls or a couple of slices of her rum cake, I'm a happy man. There's something hard about her, something regal and intimidating and strong. That strength helps me understand how a black woman could raise twelve kids in the late twentieth century in southern West Virginia.

My sister has graduated from WVU's law school, and she's having a party at Touchstone, her camp on the Greenbrier River. It's an odd mix of her husband Michael's big family, a few local white guys, my bourbon-sipping father, and a few queers: John and Laurie and me.

John and I are shoveling in the deviled eggs, potato salad, and grilled hot dogs on the back deck when I hear one man greet another around the corner, on the front porch: "Well, how you doin', ya faggot?"

I tense up, bristle, and take three steps toward the source of that hated word. "Jesus Christ!" I snarl. "I don't have to listen to that in my sister's home!"

Then I recognize the voice: a pleasant man who used the word, I am assuming, the way some men do, as a casual insult, as a joke, without any real accusation of homosexuality. Like "cocksucker." "What ya been up to, ya crazy cocksucker?" That pretense of hostility so many men use to hide their fondness for one another.

I settle down, and then I notice Mama Joyce and a few others watching me. Curiously? Apprehensively? Surely they know why John is here with me.

A few days later, my sister confesses that Tracey, one of Michael's beautiful sisters, had whispered to her, "Oh God, I could have died when Bobby said that word. He didn't mean anything by it, you know. But I'll bet Jeff hated it. It's like being called a nigger."

And that, Tracey, is one of several reasons I'm fond of you, though I don't know you well at all. The same kinds of people who hate you hate me. That creates a powerful connection.

They Show Me What I Know

The youths of any subculture ache for role models. They need to meet those who are like them but further ahead in life, productive and successful men and women who have clearly surmounted the difficulties, who have managed to get ahead in mainstream culture without assimilating, without renouncing their subculture or their true identities. Young people need to see in literature and in other forms of expression characters like themselves. Otherwise, as Adrienne Rich says in "Invisibility in Academe," "when those who have power to name and to socially construct reality choose not to see you or hear you, whether you are dark-skinned, old, disabled, female, or speak with a different accent or dialect than theirs, when someone with the authority of a teacher, say, describes the world and you are not in it, there is a moment of psychic disequilibrium, as if you looked into a mirror and saw nothing" (*Blood, Bread, and Poetry*, 199).

I remember spending my first two years in college devouring gay novels, whenever I had time outside of my English and forestry studies. Novels by Andrew Holleran, Felice Picano, and Edmund White helped me situate myself in the world and get a sense of the many ways I could choose to be gay. Though I was greatly moved by Muriel Miller Dressler's reading of her Appalachian poems at my high school in the early 1970s, and I fell in love with Maggie Anderson's poetry in graduate school, it was not until the early 1990s, when I began to come to terms with my mountain roots, that I seriously began to read Appalachian literature, and what a treasure trove it proved to be. In the novels of Lee Smith and Denise Giardina, in the poetry of James Still, Louise McNeill, and Irene McKinney, I discovered how wonderfully the region I knew could be transformed into literature.

Now, as a teacher, I have a mission when I teach Appalachian studies, Appalachian literature, or gay and lesbian literature. I introduce students to mirrors. Often undergraduates, distracted by all that young people go through in their personal lives, find it hard to make the empathic leap that literature requires. So, for God's sake, give them something they can relate to. Give a kid from Summers County a novel about the mountains. Give a young lesbian a book by Rita Mae Brown.

Jo Davison knew what she was doing when she lent me *The Front Runner*. The right books reduce alienation and banish doubt. They can be valuable ammunition against attack, confirmers and strengtheners of self.

See How Brave the Young Become

When I was young, I found role models among those older. Now, middle-aged, I am surprised by how often I come to admire the strength and integrity of the young. Future generations of Appalachian gays and lesbians, I'm beginning to believe, will more easily work their way through the stigmas and contradictions and will not feel the need to renounce one subculture in favor of another.

My ex-student Kim is a fine example of the new breed of queer youth. She was raised in a coal-mining family in the small town of Fayetteville. Entirely comfortable with her lesbian identity, she is happily coupled and has little interest in leaving the region. "I like Appalachian gay bars," Kim admitted to me. "Folk are pretty friendly around here, and, unlike the bars in cities, which often cater to a specific group of queers, West Virginia's gay bars, since they're so few, combine all the gay subcultures: men and women, younger and older, leather guys, dykes on bikes, and drag queens. It's a rich mix."

Kim also tells an unforgettable story about her years living outside the region. When she and her girlfriend moved to Florida and began socializing in a nearby lesbian bar, they were shunned as soon as the locals found out that they were from West Virginia. It turns out the other patrons took mountain-incest jokes very seriously. Since Kim and her lover were both tall and dark-haired, it was assumed that they were sisters as well as lovers!

Unlike many gay Appalachians of my generation, Kim is deeply interested in the traditions of mountain culture. As a student in my Appalachian studies class, she recognized a kindred soul and gave me such homemade treats as corn relish and such wild delicacies as creecy greens, which I promptly washed free of grit and cooked up with fatback. Kim is also passionately involved in such Appalachian controversies as the environmental effects of mountaintop mining and acid mine drainage. She wants to keep intact what little wilderness is left in West Virginia.

Everett and Glenn also give me hope. This spring John and I visited the young couple in their log cabin in southwest Virginia, which is set so high on a mountain that it's accessible only via four-wheel-drive vehicles. Everett grilled steaks, Glenn poured iced tea, and the four of us shared a late lunch on the front porch of the cabin. Far below, the north fork of the Roanoke River rushed along. Across the valley, the fog that forms after a spring rain rubbed its belly along the ridges. Just over the fence, a neighbor's herd of fat cattle grazed amidst buttercups. A mockingbird chattered somewhere, the porch wind chimes sounded. The rest was countryside silence.

Everett and Glenn are both Southwest Virginia locals: one from Patrick County, one from Alleghany County. They like their native mountains, and they intend to stay. They are part of a widely scattered circle of bear buddies they've met on the Internet, friends with whom they exchange infrequent visits. They're both out at work, though their families have adopted a "Don't ask, don't tell" policy and officially regard them as roommates. What cravings they have for big-city gay adventure they defuse with several yearly trips to bear or leather busts in Orlando, Atlanta, and New Orleans. In between those jaunts, they have that quiet mountainside to come home to. "One colleague says I have two lives," joked Everett, as he doled out slices of his homemade pie. "I'm equally comfortable at wine tastings and Wal-Mart."

It's that juxtaposition of the popular and the sophisticated, the wild and the groomed, the country and the queer, that gives one the sense of living between two worlds. John is due home soon, and I'm about to mix martinis. Some creecy greens have been simmering most of the afternoon, and the barbequed ribs are almost done. Tonight we're going to check our calendars—we have trips to San Francisco, Key West, and Lost River to schedule—then watch a DVD of Puccini's *Tosca*. Right now, however, I'm peeved, because the radio has just announced that Tim McGraw is performing at the nearby civic center this coming Saturday, but the event's sold out. The mountaineer in me loves McGraw's country music; the gay man loves his broad shoulders, furry cleavage, and handsome goatee. This double vision is the greatest gift of straddling two subcultures: the world shimmers with twice the meaning, twice the beauty.

The Shaky High Wire between Subcultures

As a young man, as I've mentioned earlier, I unconsciously patterned myself after the mountain men I grew up around, as well as my fellow forestry majors at West Virginia University. Thus my beard, boots, flannel shirts, and tattoos—a common look in the mountains, one that has fed many redneck stereotypes. Beginning as a form of protective coloration and camouflage that allowed the queer kid I was to blend in, it's eventually allowed me, as a queer adult, to define my own form of masculinity—my own peculiar combination of the wild and the groomed, the rough and the refined—and to achieve some solid sense of self, some sense of where I belong.

But this sense of belonging can be a shaky construct, and I find myself an occasional outsider in both mountain and gay communities. In most urban gay venues, my country look and country values are far from admired. In Appalachia, I'm always wondering how my fellow hill folk will feel about me when they discover that I, a bearded mountain man, am often attracted to other bearded mountain men. This is just an extreme version of what most of us ponder: Who would accept me for all that I am, even my shadowy, secret sides? Such doubt makes for painful rifts between what we are and what we appear to be. What courage it takes to suture public self to private shadow.

I almost belong here, I realized, standing with John in a corner of the San Francisco Eagle, sipping bourbon and watching bearded men in jeans, boots, and leather jackets slouching sexily by. Later, the feeling of comfort was the same, down the street at the Lone Star, a bar catering to bears. I've never fit into most mainstream gay bars, whose denizens are as unimpressed with my beard and boots as I am with their styled hair and designer clothes. But since age twenty, when I nervously slipped into Cy's, my first leather bar, a hole in the wall in Washington, DC, and found the kind of men I wanted to pursue and the kind of men I wanted to be like, I have known which gay niche is meant for me.

For a long while, the sense of belonging was limited, since for many decades such bars existed only in big cities where I was unwilling to live. Now, however, with the slow expansion of gay culture in the cities of Appalachia, I can remain in the mountains and still enjoy the company of gay men very much like me. When I watch bears and leather men march in the West Virginia Pride Parade every June in Charleston, West Virginia, I can't help but remember my youthful years of secrecy and isolation. Then I brim with amazement and gratitude, knowing that the Mountain State has, in this respect at least, changed radically for the better.

In order to achieve any sort of wholeness, we must reconcile things that look irreconcilable. Despite mainstream mockery and hillbilly jokes, I will keep my accent and cling to my regional heritage. Despite conservatives' attempts to outlaw gay marriage, I will value my relationship with John just as my heterosexual ancestors valued their marriages, and I will make that connection that many try to deny: the way I love is as valid as the way my forebears loved. John and I, at day's end, will sit down together to "high-falutin'" pleasures like martinis and Brie, then relish mountain delicacies like ramps, cornbread, fried green tomatoes, and pinto beans with chowchow. Those years of waste are over, those years unsure of my place both in the gay community and in the mountains. What difficulties that remain in living as a gay Appalachian are tensions from which I will learn, from which I will make art.

What I hope my words will do is reduce that tension for others, those who might see themselves reflected here, those who might have the strength not to retreat into an easy simplicity but rejoice instead in a difficult complexity. These poems and essays are my attempt to do what my father does every summer when he fills the pantry with home-canned garden produce, those rows of pickled beets, corn relish, tomatoes, and green beans: capturing the generosity of the earth, saving summer's gifts for hard times, preserving the past to feed the future.

I almost belong here, I realized the first time I attended the Appalachian Writers' Workshop, held every summer at Hindman Settlement School in Knott County, Kentucky. For someone as complex as I, "almost" is good enough. I loved the classes on writing and on Appalachian literature. I reveled in spending time with wonderful writers like Ron Houchin, Laura Bentley, Eddy Pendarvis, and Phyllis Moore. It was a treat to meet authors whose work I'd studied for years: Lee Smith, Robert Morgan, and James Still. And the country cooking in the cafeteria was the sort I grew up on.

For five days I attended readings and workshops there; in the evenings I sat on cabin porches playing guitar and sipping verboten bourbon, chatting with other Appalachian writers. Nevertheless I felt a strange tension, the anxiety that might be felt by a spy or imposter, or anyone else who is not what he seems. I was a little startled when a journalist noticed the rainbow rings on my baseball cap and asked me for a gay perspective on the Hindman community. Suddenly I worried that the word would get around, and wondered whether I'd still be welcome in the men's dorm. It was, fortunately, a paranoia that was to prove groundless. Country dwellers are not known for their liberal views on sexuality, but writers are.

There was one thing in particular that made me feel out of place at Hindman, that summer of 1994: I had to carefully conceal my attraction to another writer. I was single, he was handsome. How could I not look, even though the law of percentages dictated that he was straight? He stayed in the same men's dorm as I, and one day, to my pleasure, he showed up in the common room shirtless. I'm a chest man, and that morning I got the eyeful I'd hoped for, using my well-practiced peripheral vision to admire without being caught. Frustrating to see and not stroke, but what fool would touch when he knew his touch was not welcome?

Instead of touching him, I channeled that futile passion into a poem, "Wild Magnolias," a peculiar mix of Appalachian enthusiasm and homoerotic detail. Much of the literature written by gay men since 1968's Stonewall Rebellion has been frankly erotic. Perhaps we gay men write so often about desire because we have so often felt impelled to keep our desires silent. "The love that dare not speak its name," as Oscar Wilde's lover Lord Alfred Douglas put it. Certainly these days, under the Bush administration, every erotic story and poem I write and publish feels like deliberate defiance, a refusal to be silenced by our country's religious conservatism. Speaking a longing is to insist on one's freedom to feel it.

In so many circumstances, we gays and lesbians must conceal or omit what is most moving in our lives. Why, I wondered at Hindman, could I not live in a world where a straight man would take my polite appreciation of his looks as a compliment? When I wear my kilt, women are very appreciative. I am not threatened but flattered, though it is not the sort of ego food I would prefer. What fault lines in a man's sexual identity cause him to respond to erotic esteem with repulsion, threats, or violence? My lust is certainly harmless, peculiar amalgam as it is of ardor and reverence, an artist's devotion to the beautiful.

Saving What We Can

There is something enviable about inanimate objects. They feel no pain, and many of them last longer than the human body.

Today I am reminded of the persistence of possessions when I return to Hinton and find in closets my mother's abandoned clothes. In the early 1980s, reading the poetry of Sylvia Plath, I could identify with Plath's yearning for the mindless existence of things. Trapped inside her own emotional turmoil, Plath clearly wished for the solid placidity of a stone. "Is there no way out of the mind?" she asks in "Apprehensions," a question I have echoed again and again in my own bouts with depression.

There is a stateliness to gardens in winter: the tomato stakes piled against a tree, the raked leaves heaped up as mulch, the corn shocks, the bare stalks of the Brussels sprouts looking like odd South Seas totems. There is a dignity there totally lacking in a young man inside his own winter of the heart: restless, bitter, despairing, complaining, mourning, twisting about in a frantic search for some way out.

Humans are impatient, and with good reason. The earth knows it will be born again. We do not.

❦

I do not know why I am, on a quiet level rarely expressed save in my art, so obsessed with mortality. This morning it occurs to me that Candlemas, a major Wiccan holiday, is coming up in little over a week. With several writing deadlines looming, I won't be able to read a new book I've bought—*Candlemas, Feast of Flames*—in time for the celebration.

"Well," I think, watching the hopeful sun come up a little earlier than it did a month ago, "I can always get to the book by next Candlemas."

"Perhaps," says the voice of memento mori. "One never knows. Likely, but never certain. Innumerable and rarely expected, the egresses out of life. We pass them, unknowingly, every day."

This awareness is what makes monogamy problematic and fresh tomatoes with mayonnaise on my father's hot buttermilk biscuits irresistible.

How tenuous seems everything I value. When I glare at the new McDonald's in my home county, with its vulgar arches held hundreds of feet aloft, visible for miles around, or when I notice the proliferation of Wal-Marts, popping up like poisonous toadstools on the edge of every other town, or when I contemplate the environmental consequences of that modern blasphemy, mountaintop removal, it seems only logical that I, like many southerners, would glamorize and idolize the past. Despite the frequent depictions of Appalachia as a charming, static archaism, mainstream culture has swamped the mountains, and I wonder how long the native folk culture—that rich self-reliance that has taken centuries to develop—will last in the face of such onslaught.

Perhaps it can be traced to the many cats I mourned as a child, this hypertrophied concern with loss. That busy highway in front of the house on the Greenbrier River. One furry corpse after another. Some small boy inside of me has never gotten over it, and now, at age forty-five, I still brood with regularity on the evanescent nature of all I love. Midlife inevitably deepens this obsession, as I watch the world change about me—changes I never asked for, changes I deeply disapprove of—as my goatee gathers more silver, early snow in the needles of black spruce. I do my best to take no pleasure for granted. So much of poetry is simply the attempt to detain beauty.

I often speak, through the pen or the keyboard, to make sense of a shock. Whether rapturous or agonizing, the blow momentarily shatters my senses, my life, and somehow I must come to terms with it. How lucky we writers are in this respect. Others feel deeply the extremes of suffering or delight, learn from that experience—if they're wise or lucky—then move on. We writers manage to wrest from such jolts something extra: an artifact. In the face of flux, we save what we can.

Sometimes I think of art as igneous rock: cold and hard now, frozen into shape, the aftermath of fiery volcanic activity. Or an obsidian mirror, like that the Elizabethan magician John Dee used to scry the future, a mirror in which others might see themselves, albeit shadowy and distorted. Or—more of a mountain metaphor—firewood, neatly heaped fragments of someone who used to be. Flammable shards, coaxed easily into flame, radiating a welcome circle of light and warmth.

Art as firewood, lending the reader warmth? Or art as feast, feeding the reader's heart or mind? Whenever I teach literature, I feel like a parent offering dubious children a buffet of exotic food: I know it's nutritious, and my job is to convince students to taste it, despite its mystery and novelty.

Certainly the literature I have cherished has served as food. My own emotional history, as well as the history of poverty in Appalachia, reminds me of how often starvation must be endured and stoicism must be summoned. In times of past loneliness, when lovers left and friends were far away, literature fed me. Yeats, Keats; Plath, Sexton; Hawthorne, Cather, Whitman. Novels allowed me other, richer, lives; stories and essays taught me truths; poems reduced my isolation by reminding me that what I suffered had been suffered before. When the great and complex loves abandon us, there are still smaller things to grip: sun on red maple leaves, dilly beans and potato salad, a new poem to write or read.

In garden compost, every organic scrap goes to some use, and that is comforting. Coffee grounds, potato peels, the tail ends of cucumbers and tomatoes, the silver-maple leaves we raked out of the park. Even the jam and beans my Aunt Sadie put up a few years before her death, the cans that we forgot on a dusty shelf and that this afternoon I guiltily, regretfully throw out. All the work she went to, I think, but if these stale victuals can't nourish our bodies, they can nourish the soil. That is the wonderful thing about compost: its rot feeds new life.

I love recipes that use stale bread. Cajun bread pudding with rum sauce, Czech bread dumplings, croutons, English bread-and-butter pudding. Something delicious made from something an ignorant spendthrift would throw out. Such dishes remind me of art and of necessary, if often painful, introspection. Loss, rage, despair, grief: valuable emotional compost. If they are faced head-on, honestly, they can be the source of much soul refining, and certainly the fuel for most art.

Art is a form of preservative, like those polished chunks of Baltic amber in which, held up to the sun, long-dead insects can be discerned, as if suspended in honey. In poetry, I try to preserve what I am able of loveliness and longing, I try to honor those who have cared for me, I try to commemorate home. My passion for men, my loyalty to family, my attachment to landscape: these themes are inescapable.

They are long gone, that afternoon on the motorcycle, those evenings with Steve, the handsome, red-haired bartender. I remember being sixteen, gripping that nameless boy's wet belly as he drove his bike recklessly along the road high above Bluestone Reservoir. I remember being twenty-two, lighting votive candles on the dresser of that bedroom in Morgantown, West Virginia. Votives were appropriate, since what I felt was reverence when Steve shucked off his clothes, turned to me in the candlelight, beckoned, and smiled.

Erotic yearning has consumed me for years: partly lust, partly aesthetic rapture. Now in my mid-forties, married for all practical purposes, I am very far from that frightened, excited teenager on the motorcycle, that graduate student who finally held in his arms a pale and muscular man he'd wanted for months. But poetry gives us a tool with which to rescue from oblivion the fragility of what was felt. Thus, much of what I write is created for the same reasons that scholars write history books or communities erect monuments. I want to remember my lover John cooking an omelette while I read Dante; I want to remember my grandmother's big Sunday dinners; I want to remember the summer horizon over Hinton; I want to remember how loneliness felt, so as to more exquisitely appreciate my present happiness for as long as it lasts.

🦋

Once I jokingly told my sister that I want her to erect a huge black granite obelisk to mark the spot in the Ferrell family cemetery where my ashes will rest. Something impressive to greet the literary pilgrims, I said, satirizing my own leonine vanity, something majestic to make their trip worth it. "You'd better start saving for it now," Amy responded, rolling her eyes.

When I travel, I often visit the tombs of literary figures whose work I admire. Yet how much closer I feel to Sylvia Plath, reading her collected poems, than I did that summer day in England, pulling clumps of weeds from her grave mound. How much closer I feel to Henry David Thoreau, reading *Walden*, than I did visiting that cemetery in Concord, Massachusetts, or even that tiny cabin at Walden Pond.

Artists create their own tombstones. What I write will be my black granite obelisk, my very long epitaph. Words on paper are delicate, yes, but they are easily and infinitely reproducible. And when books go out of print, when a poet is forgotten? Eventually rain and wind smudge out the etchings on headstones. The result is the same: making space for other poems, other names.

New Fathoms of Thirst

Studying the simple needs of plants and animals—the tabby's canned food and warm lap, the plant's sunlight and rainwater—I often ache to escape my own complexity, my own insatiability. One of my anthems is Steve Earle's "I Ain't Ever Satisfied." Nothing is ever enough. This publication is nice, but when will the next one come? Aragorn's sword hangs on my wall; now how about his elven hunting knife? Free, I dreamed constantly of marriage's securities. Married, I occasionally yearn for bachelor independence. This restlessness is, I suspect, partly my own neurosis, partly simple human nature, and partly the yearning for the new that capitalist consumerism encourages.

Desire exhausts. It can be especially compromising and inconvenient for gays and lesbians, whose desires can alienate them from an intolerant majority. Weary of my own conflicts and hungers, I take comfort in literary evidence that others have suffered the same conundrum: the self tormented by the self. "I am tired. Everyone's tired of my turmoil," says Robert Lowell in "Eye and Tooth." "Burning burning burning burning / O Lord Thou pluckest me out" says T. S. Eliot in *The Waste Land*, echoing Saint Augustine's "caldron of unholy loves." Like Eliot, sometimes I wish to rise above the world like a mystic and be freed from desire.

I am, however, too much of a pagan and a westerner to find Eastern doctrines of transcendence very appealing. If the world is the body of God, if divinity can be found within the world rather than above or beyond it, I would just as soon believe that spiritual evolution is to be found by moving through hunger, not around it. Appetites, the body seems to suggest, are here to teach us. I prefer to find peace by living my passions, not renouncing them.

How to Live with Peace

One of the great blessings of having a spouse is being able to lay down that terrible search for touch, for romantic and erotic connection, and concentrate on the rest of the world. The spiritual sense of things, which in my bachelor days I sometimes achieved via those rare and rapturous moments with other men—Thomas, for instance, who seemed a solid manifestation of the god Pan—I now achieve in the presence of nature.

This discovery of God in the natural world—one of the great hallmarks of Romanticism—gives me yet another reason to stay in Appalachia, where nature is much easier to experience than in metropolitan suburbs. When you are visiting the tiny West Virginia village of Helvetia, contemplating the sunset on Seneca Rocks, or taking in the view from Spruce Knob, it is so much simpler finding that "still point of the turning world" that T. S. Eliot spoke of in *The Four Quartets* than it would be at the Jefferson Memorial or the Statue of Liberty, amid the noisy presence and restless shoulderings of other tourists.

My soul is like a shy fish, I have often joked. It stays in its depths when ruckus unnerves it. It only rises to the surface and is discernible and discerning when all is silent.

As much as I love to visit DC, I'm always glad to escape the Beltway chaos and begin my retreat down the Shenandoah Valley. When I exit truck-crowded Interstate 81 at Ironto, Virginia, and wend my way toward Blacksburg along tortuous back roads between hillsides of redbud, tulip tree, and sugar maple, I'm always gripped by the peace and beauty of the landscape. It is a loveliness I never take for granted. Perhaps it's because my father raised me to be a romantic in the tradition of Emerson and Thoreau. Perhaps it's because I'm in my mid-forties, happily coupled, and no longer delighted by late-night gay-bar culture. Whatever the reason, these days the company of trees, creeks, and hills feels just as necessary for my spiritual health as relationships with other human beings.

God's Bearded Face

These days I help my father in his gardens very rarely. I spend most of my spare time in Charleston with John and don't get back to Hinton as often as I'd like. When I am there, I am usually embroiled in writing, reading, or class preparation. In other words, the reluctant child I was might have been drafted into his father's projects, but the adult I am insists on focusing on projects of his own. At poetry readings these days, when I read poems about watering broccoli or digging yams, I joke that I do just enough gardening to get poems out of it, then get away as fast as possible. It's hard work, and it's my father's passion, not mine, though I have benefited from it immeasurably, not only physically with many a good meal but spiritually too.

There is a timeless, ritual quality to garden work, I realize, when I do help pick potato beetles, dig yams, or pull race weed out of the strawberry patch. Often I feel like a perpetual outsider: a gay man in a straight world, an Appalachian in an increasingly homogenous America, a Wiccan in a Christian society, a liberal in a country run by conservatives. So it feels good to believe that I belong for a time, part of a long tradition of farming, doing what my Irish, Scots, English, and German ancestors did in their own gardens. It feels good to be intimate with the earth, whose returns are often more reliable than human relationships. The cycle of the seasons, it seems to me, is the greatest poem, and a garden's metamorphoses during the course of a year vividly remind me of that poem. As a Wiccan who sees Spirit as immanent in Nature, I regard Christ's resurrection as being like that of any other sacrificed god: what was cut down in autumn's harvest leaps anew from the soil in spring.

There is quite a crowd here tonight on Redbud Ridge. We are celebrating Samhain, the ancient Celtic festival that has become today's Halloween. The circle is cast, the quarters are called, the Mother Goddess and the Horned God evoked. On a great heap of brush and wood, we burn the May pole about which we danced six months ago at Beltane. We stand around the bonfire and watch smoke and sparks rise into a starry sky, framed by the black silhouettes of wooded hills.

Wiccan in the Bible Belt. As if being gay isn't enough of a stigma. I always wonder what a local Baptist would think, stumbling on such an outdoor ceremony. Though I sometimes joke about sacrificing poodles and eating babies, especially when the former yap at dawn and the latter ruin a plane flight with their yowls, the only sacrifices consumed after a Samhain ritual would be red wine, beef stew, a green salad, and potatoes au gratin. Apple strudel would be nice too.

I owe my parents many things, but one of the most valuable was giving me the opportunity to choose my own religious path rather than forcing me to adopt Christianity. Coming out, I did not have to deal with the self-hatred and self-accusations Christian queers must grapple with. Gays and lesbians are, for the most part, welcome in neopagan faiths. We are not considered damned sinners.

He is tattooed on my left shoulder and upper arm, the face of Cernunnos, the Celtic Horned God, the face I stroked on that altar unearthed beneath Notre Dame, kept now in the Museum of Cluny in Paris. A bearded face, with stag horns that rise from his brow like flames. He is my patron deity, appropriate god-form for a devoted lover of mountains and men. He embodies forests and wildlife, the ithyphallic animal self, the hunter and the hunted, the wilderness within, the body's intoxications and ecstasies, the hairy virility of men. In him are the strength required of us by the earth's death in winter and the joy given us by the earth's newborn green.

The Silver in My Beard

August 1977, and I'm packing for college, stuffing the suitcases my parents got me for my high school graduation present. Much to my mother's delight, I've cut off the long, hippie hair I've worn for years. I've also grown a beard: black, with faint red highlights, a legacy from the Irish blood, perhaps. The beard's a little patchy, but it will be enough to create a new image, to give a new impression when I get to Morgantown. I'm tired of being who I was in high school. I don't want to be a celibate scholar obsessed with getting straight As. I want to be someone else in college. My body and my heart are as eager for education, experience, and development as my brain.

College will be my first extended foray into the world by myself, so I have to take Joni Mitchell's travel album *Hejira* with me. And a copy of *The Front Runner*, just to reread every now and then. And my denim jacket, which I pull out of my bedroom closet. I shake it out, hold it up, and begin to fold it.

Then I notice the tiny holes in the back of the jacket, and I'm reminded of why I'm so eager to leave my hometown. When I read *The Front Runner* in my junior year, I discovered that the gay liberation movement had adopted the Greek letter lambda as its symbol. When my friends Bill and Kaye preceded me in escaping to WVU, they'd reported that many men in the gay bar there wore denim jackets. So I bought a denim jacket and asked my friend Sally to stitch a lambda on it. She had laboriously done so, in lavender thread.

I wore that jacket to high school for a week or two before I realized that, if I could find out that the lambda represented gay liberation, so too could others in Hinton. Suddenly that letter on the back of my denim jacket felt like a target, a bull's eye. One night with a pair of scissors I picked all the threads out. The lavender lambda disappeared, inch by inch. An act of cowardice, a self-maiming, a necessity.

Today, I take the jacket with me to college, just as a reminder of why I can never live in Hinton again. I want to find a place where I can be both safe and honest.

Today I am learning to be safe. Today, George "Dubya" Bush has announced his support of a constitutional amendment opposing gay marriage, and I am attending a meeting of the Virginia Tech boxing club for the first time.

I haven't done anything even resembling this since the late 1970s, since those three phys ed classes in college—self-defense, karate, and aikido—none of which I was particularly skilled in. In fact, I used to joke to undergrad friends that I'd learned just enough of the martial arts to make myself dangerous to myself. From Sensei Boyd, I learned how to brandish a fistful of car keys, how to punch and kick, how to roll, how to dance through a few katas, but the practice, after those classes ended, lapsed into theory and fading memory.

For years—despite my hot temper, despite the semireasonable paranoia that being queer in America inspires—I have been putting it off, this fresh attempt to learn how to protect myself. Between teaching, traveling back and forth between Blacksburg and Charleston (with occasional weekends with my family in Hinton), and trying to write, revise, and publish, I have barely enough time to get to the gym to lift weights with any regularity. True, I've talked to a couple of black belts about perhaps taking some private lessons, I've read information about martial arts classes here in Blacksburg, and I've read a few books on the warrior archetype and relished a lot of action movies. But I'm still the leather-jacketed, booted, hillbilly/queer English professor who's good at striking a brooding, gray-bearded-biker pose (patchwork quilt of carefully constructed identity, masculinity as defensive barricade), but doesn't have much of an idea of how to implement his anger, of how to protect himself, his family, or his friends by kicking some attacker's ass if circumstances demand it. "Open up a can of whup-ass," as my students put it. It's an expression I savor.

I have taught at Virginia Tech, as a fairly open gay man, since 1989, but only recently have I felt threatened. First, Karen DePauw was hired for an important position at Virginia Tech, but her lesbian partner, Shelli Fowler, was, at the last minute, refused a spousal-hire position by members of the board of visitors, who then, several months later, removed gays and lesbians from the list of groups protected against discrimination on campus. The public outcry was so loud that the board of visitors relented, reversing both actions.

But now I am working for tenure, publishing lots of queer material and even some gay erotica; some swine has complained to Virginia Tech alumni chapter presidents about the openly gay nature of my website; and the president of the United States has declared his opposition to gay marriage. I am anxious and I am angry, and my boyfriend has bought me a punching bag and gloves for Christmas. I want to learn how to use them.

The boxing coach is a friendly man with a thick local accent who makes me entirely welcome, even though, with this silver-streaked beard of mine, I am clearly out of place, over twenty years older than any of his other aspiring boxers. The kids adore him, it's clear. He knows all their names and asks about their lives as he wraps up their hands and helps them on with their gloves.

I watch a while—admittedly admiring a few young bits of scenery. (To adapt a previous phrase of mine, "I'm ethical, boys, I ain't blind!") Coach finally gets around to wrapping and gloving me, then gives me some basic directions—"Turn your hands this way. Okay, that's good. No, now, keep your hands up! Twist your wrist about here. It's the torque that produces the power."

Waiting for my turn on a bag, I study the young boxers' efforts, trying to learn what I can from guys who obviously know what they're doing. Lots of muscular, athletic-looking white guys, of course. But, unusual for mostly Caucasian Virginia Tech, there's quite a multicultural mix in this room. A few Asian American boys, a few African American boys, a couple of African American girls, a Middle Easterner or two. Plus a decent number of white boys who are small framed or short. Then there's me, the German/Scots/Irish/English American queer. I wonder how many of these kids come here for the same reason I have: because they might feel a little marginalized, a little at risk.

Then it's my turn on the punching bag. Five two-minute rounds, one one-minute round, then thirty seconds of constant pummeling. I dance around the bag, trying to implement the coach's advice, hoping I don't look entirely foolish, entirely incompetent (every man's worst nightmare). I'm slamming as hard and fast as I can and imagining their faces—the hateful preachers and politicians, gay-bashers past and future—muttering "Son of a *bitch!*" under my breath.

"Work! Work now!" Coach shouts, and I punch even harder, determined not to look weak or lazy in front of these built young men, who are jumping rope or working their own bags and so probably not even noticing me. In between rounds, I sweat and suck in air, a little lightheaded, hoping I don't faint or have a heart attack, regretting every extra Yuletide-, Candlemas-, or Valentine's Day–inspired belly inch, wishing I'd come to this sport twenty years ago. How much different might my life have been with the underlying security, the daily physical confidence, this sport surely provides?

Coach yells, "Relax!" but that, and pacing myself, will come later, with any luck and with persistence. Right now, I'm going for strength, not speed or skill. I want that bag to swing crazily. I want to break through that carefully inculcated barrier that civilization palisades around each of us: "*Don't hurt, don't break. Rein in.*" I want the strength and skill to protect what I love and to destroy what needs destroying.

❦

A rainy autumn day, and John and I are visiting my family in Hinton. Daddy shows me his new conservative-skewering editorial, Amy tells me about her new court case, and I preen about my latest published poem and my boxing semiprowess (always, always, the son's attempts to make the father proud). John sits quietly, observing the family dynamics he's grown accustomed to during our years together. Only my mother's absence makes the scene incomplete.

This afternoon we're transferring to the basement innumerable jars of produce that Daddy and Amy have canned. Later, we'll have a fire—John loves a wood fire, and Lord knows I've had enough practice making them, though I might have to split some kindling first. This evening I'll start a new novel by Edmund White, one of my favorite gay writers, or get some Appalachian studies class preparation done, or maybe waste some time fingerpicking a few Tim McGraw or Joni Mitchell songs on the guitar.

Now, as we fill boxes with canned vegetables, I think about how much I enjoy returning to Hinton to see my family and to admire the beautiful landscape, the conjunction of mountains and river and sky. I think about how much I've changed, how much my hatred of the region has diminished and how much my love and my confidence have grown. Home, once the place I fled, has become the place I come to flee the world. A change well worth the silver in my beard, the furrows in my brow, my increasingly weighty history. It is the blessing of hardship, this deepening appreciation of kin: facing adversity side by side, passing sustenance hand to hand, creating safety and shelter against whatever cold may come.

Six
Poems

Splitting Chestnut Oak

We upend the logs,
set the wedges, swing
the maul. Sap bubbles
about the sinking steel
with each metal ching.
The slow cracking builds,
the yield of fibers
that intertwined years
and now mere seconds force
apart. Somewhere beneath
our breastbones we know
how this feels. Steel rives
our selves, the fissures
splintering slowly
beneath rhythmic blows
down our spines, along
ribs, femurs, finger ends
into the earth as unerring
as lightning. Let someone
who hates waste redeem
these fragments from wet rot.
Let the heartwood, if
it must be split, be burnt
in its ruin, only warm
some lonely brother's hearth.

Bluestone Reservoir

It must have been Riunite,
beginner's wine, that first
summer out of college.
Down by the Bluestone Reservoir,
we got drunk fast, immersing
ourselves in the jade of June,
stripping to the waists, sprawling
across car hoods. Manhood first
was how long a gulp you took, as
the sun brewed musk in the rich
black grass across our chests,
our bellies, between our legs.
In the sweet sweat of wine
and folly I agreed:
my first motorcycle ride, a boy
I hardly knew, whose name's
still submerged like abandoned
farms in the reservoir's waters.
He kicked and gripped, I slid on,
we rode along the sandstone
road cuts, dodging the after-rain
rock slide scatters. His belly
was lean and wet and bare beneath
my hands, he yelled into the wind
"Hold tight!" and I was grateful
for any excuse to clutch.

Allen

On the first wood gathering of autumn,
in forest that was once cornfield,
slopes so rocky instead of wagons
sleds were used, my father and I
find the remains of a split-rail
fence his grandfather set a century ago.
American chestnut, brittle, stiff,
resistant to rot—fine kindling
now, to start spark beneath
the red oak we will split today.
Soon the garden will be blackened,
the ponds too iced for geese,
home forgather around the flame
we insure this afternoon.

The stature of the chestnuts
he holds in my father's memory.
Allen towered with them, rooted
like Antaeus, fell soon after
those giants dwindled and left
across Appalachia their stubborn stumps.

What does a man like a chestnut tree
leave behind? My middle
and my family names. A white oak
maul, handle smooth with use.
Froe-split shingles to keep the cold
rains off. Scars in the sides
of sugar maples, scattered fence
rails. And a grandson who shows
his son how to split fallen oak
with maul and wedge, how to carve
elderberry twigs into sugar-water spiles.
How to love mountains fiercer
than any marriage. From the stuff
of graves how to seed and coax

birth after birth after birth,
with simmered syrup how to sweeten
loss and the daily biscuit, from
the death of trees how to keep
the heart's hearth alive.

How to dissolve as even chestnut
stumps one day must, or the rails'
brief andiron flame. How to
dissolve like farm-pond ice
in March, its cracks and edges
and pockmarks lost, clenched
atoms relaxing into spring.

West Virginia Towns

Beartown, Plum Orchard, Pickle Street.
Big Ugly, Cornstalk, Cyclone.
Romance, Paradise, Odd.
Aurora, Paw Paw, Mount Storm.
Wildcat, Bear Heaven, Helvetia.
Burnt House, Hominy Falls, Hurricane.
Apple Grove, Cucumber, Crab Orchard.
Bob White, Elk Garden, Frost.
Mud, Mount Hope, Sam Black Church.
Sweet Springs, Snowshoe, Beelick Knob.

Luckily, the legends are often true.
In every West Virginia town,

there are men like me, men
with beards, baseball caps, pickup trucks,
whose boot treads tramp in mud
and oak chips, who howl the Mountaineers
to another pigskin victory.

Women like my sister, who
armload in the split wood,
lug bushels of freshly dug
potatoes to the basement.

And in a house in each one
of these towns, where morning
glories string sapphire along the porch,

an elderly woman's soaking a pot
of pinto beans, or cooking half-runners
with fatback all afternoon, rolling out
short crust for fried apple pies,
kneading smooth a batch of biscuit dough,
just as my grandmother did for seventy years.

Lemon Cake

Young. So young,
that patina of sheet lightning
danced over bus rides, interstate
median strips. An autoharp
drew shivers, a pasture-roaming
collie respect, lemon cake
devotion. I gripped you then,
moraine of Victoriana, deaf
guardian of a favorite niece's
child. Of that generation of doilies

and hairnets, the oppressive crimson
of velvet drapes, elderly homes
where I drew to the bone,
beneath thought, that old lady love
free of men's conditions, father-criticisms.
Where I lured rabbits to propped
boxes with sugared carrots,
where I learned to speak slowly
and feast southern well, rocking on
firefly porches, with water hand pumped
splashingly from the gifting ground.

You dissolved like sugar crystal,
one last wave from the window
of a rest home in Fairlea.
Today, Great-aunt Grace, I am home.
My mother, who claims to be no cook,
after dinner serves lemon cake,
icing almost imperceptibly pink,
a rippling genealogy
of recipe. One bite, and
a score of summers lapses away,
humming and purling with
sugar and citrus, a creek smoothing
pebbles, a hand proffering fireflies.

See how you sweeten us yet.

Tomato Stakes

Old man Huffman split these, twenty years
ago, one Summers County autumn, his breath
condensing for a scarf, the Greenbrier
smoothing over its jade, cutting between
bank willows into the trough of winter.
The year Huffman's heart insisted
he sit down, my father bought them all
with a promise, swearing neither would
ever want for tomatoes again.

A country bargain kept: every August,
green tomatoes fried in sugared cornmeal,
like oysters shot through with chlorophyll.
Sunday morning biscuits heaped with mayonnaise
and red slabs. Each summer ending in tomato
generosities: canned whole, or juiced, or
simmered into spaghetti sauce; still fresh,
mulch-stained, snuggled into shoeboxes in
the nomadic bed of a pickup truck, Ball jars
to warm me through another bachelor winter.

Sun-bright on pine, evocations of wood
smoke, this autumn, regular as the receding
of sap, and across Appalachia the same
hillside hands gather in the tomato stakes.
These saviors are withered to the root, tied
to sacrificial posts with baling twine,
faces to the earth, leaning limp along
the Appian Way, their chartreuse psalms
drained off by some spider of late frost.
Like lovers parting, they will stand for a while
from habit, all support gone, then sink
without excuse into sweet diffusions of mulch.

Our pocketknives shear the twine, we shoulder
shake and heave up stakes, the mud falls back.
Amidst amber intricacy beneath the pine,

leaning together about the trunk, flying
buttresses of locust, an antique arsenal
of spears. Impervious, they will withstand winter,
the pine sough and Pleiades sifting about them,

while our bodies unknit whispering, another winter
hardens our veins. Crystals of uncertain
entropy, snow will skirl about them mimicking
May, as they dream of spring, soft
penetrations. As they remember the roots
from which they were split, the whole
axed from their flanks, noble even in shards,
hoarfrost whitening the rough grain of dawn.

Goldenrod Seeds

complete the decade beyond your death.
Stemmed flumes of river fog, pasture fog,

these gray gauntlets lining December's
mountain back roads, lining the family

graveyard's link fence. Feasts are what
I remember most, dinner tables where

good food was love made solid,
offered by those too shy or proud to speak it—

buttermilk biscuits and country ham,
cobblers rich with blackberries

thicketing the dell below the cemetery.
I brought daisies, your favorite flowers,

to your deathbed, then tried
to forget what you said—

a dream in which you died,
and what woke you was not fear

of death but worrying
how afterwards I might survive.

No one knows which breath is last
until that breath is over,

as if silence defines
all that came before.

We men who are too stern,
we carry the weight of each refused tear

like stones. Our hearts are leather
bags slowly filling with river-smooth gems—

agate, smoky quartz, snowflake obsidian.
We own our griefs, will not let go,

for sorrow is solid, something to hold hard,
to stroke, remembering gifts given by those

we have lost. Grandmother, I brush
winter leaves from your marker. I puff

a seeding stalk of goldenrod out
along the wind—its gray trails match

my breath, your breath rising, heat
from subsiding, shimmering sunlight.

Each seed a breath,
each breath a stream of stars.

Digging Potatoes

Toxic odors of Jimson weed.
Ragweed's gold dust, pokeweed's garnets,
foxtail dew. Amidst all this useless
richness, we seek out the final
hills. Fogs of the equinox fumble
over pastures, spiral over ponds,
settle like eerie birds in the walnut
boughs already bare. We have come
for the last gifts of the dying.

Look for shriveled limbs. Then fork
beneath those consumptive splays, lift
and shake. What parts poisonous,
what parts edible—for that knowledge,
the past paid, for these safe harvests.
Gold buried does not bud, corpses
do not sprout, tendrils breaking
from fingertips and crawling towards
the light. Only potatoes. And memory.

Today we are archaeologists,
psychoanalysts, digging the dark lobes
for something lost long ago to force
our blood-fires through the snow.
Irish ancestors shove through my shoulders,
curse the tuber caught on a tine, the bushel
handle cutting its load into the palm.
Against heart's famine there is
no proof. Against the belly's,

potato cakes, Dublin coddle, colcannon,
chowder. We hum, exhumations over,
one hunger we can hoard against,
hefting baskets to the basement.
Now we need a little less.

Ramps

It's a craving at this point.
Mid-April, the hand-lettered signs
show up on country storefronts, roadside stands.

I seize the last decent batch
from the bottom of a cooler at Capitol Market.
"You'll reek for three days!"

my grandmother used to warn,
but it's only onion apocalypse
if you eat them raw, I promise.

In the sink I shake off forest mulch,
black mountain earth, I trim off the hydra-
headed roots, dirty diaphaneity of outer skin,

then rinse the leaves, so like lilies
of the valley my mother grew once
by the Greenbrier River, within a grove

of pines. Chopped coarsely, they pop
and sizzle in the bacon fat before I add
sliced potatoes, patience, scrambled eggs,

then finally taste that earthy, spicy, garlic edge.
We love ramps because they're rare, only once a year,
taking spring's evanescence between our teeth

after months of hillside pewter, hoarfrost pasture,
paralyzed ponds, breathing gray
in and out, in and out. We love them because

ramps remember the wild asleep
beneath our skin, a rich green wild
we hungrily take in and taste again,

while another Wal-Mart goes up,
another well runs dry, draglines slice off
the breast of another mountaintop.

Turnip Greens

Up Pie Holler now
the New England asters are
lavender, funereal,
the hickories drip with topaz.
In the evening's still and smoky
quartz you hear far down
the hillside a car rattle
loose bridge planks above
the river's brier green.
You point out Venus
to a grandchild.

For the jars of apple butter
mother after mother after mother
simmered, dark hands spooning
out cinnamon, sorghum or sugar,

for the pot of turnip greens
steaming woodstove top
with hog jowl all afternoon,

for the quilts vigorous retirement
sews—log cabin, bear
paw, wedding ring—

many thanks. The chrysanthemums
are crackling electric, the maple
leaves loose their fingers' grip,
relinquish long security for
the briefest flame. All
the food and fuel and warmth
our hands provide, living

and dying and after. Smooth down
that child's haphazard hair,
shove hands to the wrists

in roll yeast-dough,
spoon up another bowl of greens.
Our bones like deep roots with
the seasons sleep and ache and sleep.
Turnip greens turn earth
to bone, bone scrimshawed,
the delicate trace of fossil fern,
mountain melting into muscle melting

into mountain. So many gifts
hold us here. The blessed
never leave for long,

as last spring's leaves and last
year's grass only feed the humus
of hillsides. Home, the first
fragile grip of seeds.

Creecy Greens

Christmas shopping in Roanoke I saw them,
sandy spiders for sale in the farmers' market,
a treat few outside Appalachia would recognize.

From the barren flats above the cliffs,
those riverbank rocks time raised to mountainside,
you gathered creecy greens, age and autumn
stiffening your spinster stoop. Over the sink
you hunched them, rinsing off grit.
How long they simmered I do not know,
the shy child I was choosing the affections
of moss and oak, the elfin fancies of ferns.

Like the Mann farm, slopes too steep for surplus,
you were too stern for me, slapping my back
your only touch, made formal by poverty.
Perhaps you thought me weak, loving
books over gardens as I did. I preferred
the Ferrells, my father's other family branch,
all the abundance that permits warmth,
the closest to landed gentry West Virginia ever had,
huge bottomland farms portioned off
and lost long before the deed descended to me.

As you died long before my manhood,
long before I knew how few are arable bottomlands
or any abundance, how the sediments of solitude
may silt up a life span like yours or mine,
the way a small pond slowly fills with sedges
and cattails. It is your mountain blood that allows
this endurance, as I clean meticulous a batch
of creecy greens, snow blowing in again beyond
the steamed window panes. I am strong enough now,
boxing away a silver ring, raking leaves off graves
as frost seizes the limbs, as silver petals
in my weary beard. This skill you embodied:

how to live on weeds, how the wilderness feeds us
if we know which plants to pluck. How to season
spareness with fatback, how rich pot liquor is:
with home-baked biscuits we sop up every drop.

Chowchow

Save for the spices—celery seed,
mustard seed, cinnamon and cloves—

my father's grown it all: cabbage
plump enough to fill a lap,

green bell peppers' shredded jade,
the red cayenne and Hungarian hot

arching inside like cathedral naves
carved from ruby, intense to eye and tongue,

the High Romantics of the garden.
Come morning-glory season

he puts it up, that regional oddity from
a better America, before McDonald's

and strip malls swallowed the cornfields.
Chowchow tastes like childhood,

like ancestry, and so we cherish it,
summers stalled behind Ball jar glass.

Our future's a bowl of beans—
cranberry, pinto, yellow eye—

simmered with bacon grease,
steaming the winter windows,

served with hot corn bread, black sorghum,
a jar of chowchow brought up from the basement.

Dilly Beans

On the last dog day, frantic
last-minute phone calls in search
of dill weed. Violently red co-op
cayenne pepper. Smelly hot
vinegar, the generosity of garlic.

I return from a walk to find them
already canned, the Blue Lakes
I helped plant and pick: green
columns in brine, sunken cities,
crunchy finger bones I will snap
delightedly between my teeth

on those lucky winter evenings
I am home and my sister chooses
to dole them out. This August
afternoon we sit about the kitchen
smiling, lifting gin and tonics
to abundance, to Ball jar autonomy,
waiting for the seals to pop.

Civilization Comes to Summers County

On a metal tower ten stories high
the golden arches gleam.

How long did our town council woo them
before they deigned to come?

The first McDonald's in Summers County,
West Virginia. The usual classic fare—

what could be more American?—
plus intestines in neon red and orange,

huge curving pipes shrieking children slide through,
like manic hamsters, proctologists' probes.

Our grandparents used to gather ramps
and creecy greens, boil down sorghum,

can tomatoes, peppers, chowchow, beans.
Who needs all that now?

Against the Alleghenies' October smolder,
against the sky's sapphire, that monstrous

yellow *M* humps, visible for miles.
Every morning, out back,

the garbage heaps: cups, wraps,
the little Styrofoam coffins

whose fatty innards were gobbled yesterday.
Down the road, amidst eager yellow jackets,

crab apples ripen,
drop to the sidewalk, rot.

Sawing, the Last Day of Winter

Craving a Miller Lite for lunch, he gleans
an early tan, thickening his calluses,

snuffling ends of black birch's rural
wintergreen, listening to distant trains

and their smoky evocations of escape.
Rough limb bark bare against bare

chest, sawdust drifts in his belly hair
like dust in roadside webs.

A cat sleeps in the warm leaves under
the porch, spring cresses bloom white

motes beneath his feet. The peonies' first
fingertips have decided another prayer

is worth the effort, and so the dead arise
in bud smoke, blood-ruddy as rake trails

the saw teeth well along his forearm.
Pack the boots and the thermal underwear up,

sleep naked, save wood for next year.
Another winter over, hunger still intact.

Walking in Night Fog

The way streetlights striding through
the left leaves of red maple grow holy in fog—
a child thinks of crowns of feathers.

I know these nights best, their wet densities,
and later their dread, balancing on lines of silence,
avoiding the dripping clutch of locust boughs.

Somewhere, I know, people are sitting with tea
and television, behind their windows
in the light they pay for,
          some looking out on fog.

A numbness of the air.
The lights of the valley feed into distance.
Nothing means as much.

This is the feeling of a stone submerged
          in week-old rainwater,
that sudden sheet of glass,
          meeting an old lover before a restaurant
          by accident,
too shocked to absorb the red mustache,
          the dusty crab apple leaves.

Now only a stranger passes, another fog walker.
What has damned him?
In what is left of the face,

in the moonlight   his lips move.

Weeds

Pray for them, these displaced seeds—
the jimson weed, toxic thorn apple
bristling the barnyard; amidst
the rows of strawberry and corn,
the lamb's quarter, the race weed,
the amaranthus, velvet leaf
and crabgrass. We bend and tug,
we shake the roots free of soil
and toss them cursing in a ditch.

"God, won't you open up?"
The bare back is turned toward you
in bed, broad shield; arrows,
the clatter of words subside.
As if such a fortress could be forced.
Your hand reaches across the dunes
of sheet, hovers inches
from a shoulder, retreats. The weakness
of the slowly starved. Rain is pooling
across concrete, shuddering the prisms
of oil. A little light left falls
across a vase of paper flowers.

Some demon sows them, the seeds
of weeds, all things rooted
where they are not wanted.

The Harvest of Motes

Brushing crumbs to the
edge of the plate,

moistening a finger,
drawing them up.

Every lifespan will know
this harvest of motes,

when a handshake, a word,
another's leavings,

when not enough
must be

enough, and the sigh
of thanks for

this much, this much, this much.

Over Country-Fried Steak the Adulterer Retires

Hours lined with icefall
along the Massachusetts Turnpike.
What remains is asphalt
stained with salt, lined with
stretched, never-ending subtractions,
the powerlessness of hands
to hold what refuses keeping.

In the Friendly's parking lot,
Hazleton, Pennsylvania, a man
still clutches the steering wheel,
listening to the cooling engine's clicks.
Like the slowing juice-beat of bugs
in summer's truck grates,
groans at the eaten edge of continents.
Loosening, the interlocked fingers where
petiole meets twig, rainstorm acids meet stone.

When he enters the restaurant, he splits
in half: the boy in him stares at the chalked
special with glee, the man takes up
a corner table far from people and watches
March demand its drizzle. There is always
this numbness after meeting necessity.
He has explained, he has wept
in his lover's lap, he has excused all
he cannot hold and lopped his clawing
fingers off. He has lied one last time,
loaded up his luggage, from a mendacious
ecstasy begun his exile.

Grief is all didactic, redefinition,
the shards of an isosceles triangle.
Still the mazed man cannot help but smile,
watching the grateful delight with which
the child feasts: country-fried steak

and buttered corn and biscuits and
a sundae included free! So many kinds
of starvation. This drive begins another.
Oblivious, the boy sops milk gravy
with biscuit, the man shakes his head,
stares at the ceiling streamers,
the stream of rainy pane, and sighs—
"I wanted more than food for us.
I tried, child. I tried." The boy
looks up and smiles: the sundae has arrived.

Ambush

The lovelorn are ambushed
by the tiniest things.
The seminal trail of snails
across concrete, rosebuds

probed open by the sun's summer tongue.
The name "Taylor" on a tombstone,
the way a passing stranger seems
to have stolen a long-departed brow.

About the abandoned graveyard,
fed by the dead, the maple leaves
blaze with grace, burnt orange
in the fire of their dying.

The bodies we love
leave us at last, and then
become inescapable.

Amidst autumn's embers
and ashes, dilapidated
the stranded sing—

How long, how long,
how much longer

must we pay
for joy?

Maple Syrup

The masking tape on the jar lid says
1973. Heaviest snow in my memory—
about the house the heap of two feet,
exhausting the flexible spruce,
so we mix buttermilk into buckwheat flour
and from a cellar cupboard after twenty years
retrieve this long-forgotten jar.

At fourteen maple syrup was nothing special,
something everyone else must be accustomed to,
and too much work. Wearisome, lugging zinc
buckets of sugar water down the wintry
hills, gathering wood for the fire.
And so little yield—from forty gallons
of dripped sap one meager gallon's syrup.
I expected more sweetness from the world,
bliss uncoaxed, not distilled with long effort
and one's own roughened hands. I knew
worth would accrue results, honorable love
in all justice would be returned.
It was a relief to shut down the sugarhouse:
I had easier things to do.

Amidst the crystalline ruins of winter,
one West Virginian manhood, I pour
what I recognize now as costly, as precious,
a few tablespoons from that small jar,
that last jar, onto a pile of gritty, sad
buckwheat cakes. I bite into this history:

those mornings split between winter and spring,
when sun against the maple flanks conjures up
the sap's ascent. All that charcoal-gray silence
in the sugar grove, a flicker rapping remotely.

About me the tiny plink   plink   plink.
Siphoned up roots from the mountains' rocky flesh,
the rain and groundwater some alchemy in maples
makes sweet. Dripping from spiles of elderberry
in summer broken and carved, freed of pith. Each drop
ignited by early sun trembling pendant on the spile
lip before the silver shudder and fall. Zinc buckets
propped on sandstone stoops my great-grandfather set,
the bark pocked with vague scars he drilled
in the Februaries of another century.

We stayed up late, simmering the great oblong pan,
skimming off the scummy froth, sitting long
on banks of windfall limbs, searching
for the Pleiades, between which branches they nested,
searching out certainties in the North Star,
stretching chill-stiff palms as if in hope of
lasting blessing towards the fire. Even the air was sweet.

        2

I lick the last drops of maple syrup from my lips,
knowing again a mustache moist with manna beneath mine,
ecstasies after which so much is merely wait.
A face still vague with sleep is dwindling
in the seconds between doorjamb and door.
Matched mysteries, eyes meet. On mumbled goodbyes
the door closes with a switchblade snick.
Years lost, a bliss too brief to be jarred and sealed.
I finger-scrape the last sweet crumbs from the plate,
taste a body memory has finalized as Michelangelo
did marble, as my great-grandfather's memory
held some woman's body long loved.

The long evaporations, the patience, years
of simmering off, the distillation of decades.
Some syrup is consumed in a season. We are left
with sticky fingers and lips, satisfied with nothing
less, knowing how paltry all attempts
to preserve so intense a sweet.

Cornfield in March

Winter's nuclear sleet has leveled this field.
One thinks of cities in the dawn of
the bomb's aftermath, or a man studying his own
face the first night alone, after the funeral.

I walk through the fallout, envying such
unmitigated desolation. Appalachian beard
stubble, a battleground of bones,
bones the color of amber exhausted, a few
skeletal patriots still standing, clinging
to clods with their tepee clutch of roots.

The cobs, machine clean, scatter like pagan
sanctities, rough phalli, idols thrown down,
all their gems stolen, sprawled amidst
the topaz lanterns of the horse nettle,
the careless dung of deer.

Wild Magnolias

1. Folk

"Community, not competition," so I've heard.
I am, as my great-grandmother used to put it,
juberous, but there it is, waiting over the wooden bridge,
on the far side of Troublesome Creek. High-summer season,
wild magnolia bloom. For five days I almost belong.

There's Ron with his pipe smoke and Galway tales,
Dana and Rita, Eddy and Laura reading graceful verse.
There's Phyllis reading her PIWASH essay, claiming West Virginians
are Yankees! "Madam," I intone, pulling about me
the gray wool of my last life, "We're all southerners in Summers
     County,"
then add her to my short list of much-loved northerners.

There's Marie, slipping a teaspoon of illegal bourbon into her Coke.
Now I know Blanche Dubois proclaimed that "a shot never does a
     Coke
any harm!" but a teaspoon? "Why bother?" I quiz her.
"That's what my husband says!" she replies, sipping daintily,
so I christen her Mizz Bibulosity, tap her glass with mine,
then slip onto the porch to light a cigar and suck down my Dickel
     straight.

2. Feasts

Knott's dry, I'd heard, and by God, it is.
In the local convenience store, I can't even find that fizzy amber water
that passes for beer in most of America. Imagine, if you will,
a thirsty crew of Southern writers, mountain writers, with only
sulfur water and lemonade to drink, and you'll understand prayer,
you'll comprehend canonization, how cross-the-county-line smugglers
     evolve into saints.

The cooks of Hindman Settlement School are angelic already,
setting out spreads worthy of the hillbilly afterlife, the down-home
toothsomes my grandmother used to make. Fried chicken, smoky

brown beans, corn bread, turnip greens, and pies, pies,
the simplest happiness: apple, cherry, salacious coconut cream.

Then there's that verboten feast denied the tongue,
which only shy eyes can stroke. Suddenly that grad student sleeping
just down the hall makes me wish I worked in silver nitrate, not
    syllables,
makes me wish that words could carve solids like sculptors.
Could recreate, possess, perpetuate the baby face, the short brown
    beard,
baggy T-shirt falling off a shelf of pecs. Daybreak in the men's dorm,
he stands yawning, bare chested and barefoot, in the tousled luck
of morning light. How I envy the sun its liberties. Its clover-honey
    tongues
lap a torso lightly muscled, the moss-swirl of nipple fur, that ridge
of belly hair descending. Hungry celibate, I stare, then look politely
    away,
edging along the shaky high wire between subcultures.

    3. Forests

Last evening at Hindman, and over the valley
a storm sweeps in, breaking weeks of drought.
We gather on the hillside porch, where someone lights candles,
someone tunes a guitar and begins to play "The Water is Wide."
Our voices join with theirs, generations nameless, long dead,
singing, "Love is gentle, and love can be so kind,
the reddest rose when first it's new." Night falls with the rain,
rain driving down hard, filling the withered creek.
None of us has wings, and our song is ending now,
but the storm continues past us. We sit silent
in the welcome sound of it, the drumming on roofs,
the dripping off leaves and eaves. About us,
the trees steam, growing vague with mist,
wild magnolia blossoms gleam like faces in the forest dark.

The Cosmopolite and the Convict

Here you are, after
    the white heather of Glencoe,
        the covered bridges of Lucerne,
    St. John's cave on Patmos,
        Dun Aengus and the cliffs of Moher,
    the throne room of Knossos,
        the chapel of Versailles,
Notre Dame, Brussels, London, Berlin, Vienna, Ephesus.

Here you are, after
    God knows how many books,
        a smattering of foreign languages,
    fine wines and ales, a passion
        for Puccini, a collection of diplomas,
    ethnic cookbooks, mounting publications,
        a burgeoning CV.

Here you are in Huntington, West Virginia,
    stepping out onto the columned porch
of the Congregational Church
    in the season of first crocuses and silver-maple bloom.
The taste of communion's pale and dry as paper,
    your body's the last lingering snow drift. Winter
in the blood, marrow, muscle, skin,
    winter that will not end.
A flicker in the distance is drumming hard
    for simple food, while you, cosmopolite,
stare at moving muscles, a bare chest and shoulders,
    buttocks curving beneath burnt-orange sweatpants.
A convict's shooting hoops behind barbed wire,
    behind the Cabell County courthouse,
across the spring-windy street.

Mizz Alice

Straight from Jewell Ridge, Mizz Alice
is versed: how to string shucky beans,
how to cook pork chops, breaded and fried,
with peppery gravy and buttermilk biscuits.
After dinner I push back from the table,
unbutton my jeans, wipe my beard and sigh.

She knows the same weather signs as I:
the ring around the moon, silvery leaves
turning over, the way chimney smoke hovers,
how cattle lie down in pasture before noon.
What delights her is azalea, its flesh-
pink bonfires about a house of her own,

or the way deer step out in moonlight
to browse beneath straggled pear trees,
to leave their prints in the stipple
of fallen bird seed loud blue jays scattered.
With a jar of apple butter, a loaf of nut bread,
she warms the winters of friends and kin,

and when we've all had enough of cold, when
we ache for those lawn chair days beneath
pear shade, for summer gin, juleps and tobacco,
she remembers what as a child she was told
about unmelted snowbanks left lying, pitted
with cinders or salt, but holding on still

in blue shade beneath hemlock or spruce.
Such a relic is waiting like grief for more snow
to join it. So to hell with the groundhog.
Alice boils up a stew pot of water, marches down
the drive, and—conjurer of coltsfoot, dogtooth violet—
pours hot water over snow, woe's last dirty trace.

Sunday Sunlight

I want to romanticize those years alone:
moors I strode across in high storm,
Inverness cape swirling about my shoulders,

or heather-wild Highland glens and braes
I roamed among, sword at the ready,
nights wrapped in my tartans

by a dying fire pit. These alter egos
must make it obvious: actually,
the tragic hero simply read a lot—

isn't a good book better than most days,
most company? I did buy a kilt,
a dirk, an onyx ring, just to borrow

the trappings of drama denied.
I worked late, played guitar, listened
to Wagner and Puccini, visited kin

on the weekends, went to Europe once a year.
In the gym, I ached for younger, better bodies,
then trudged home to empty rooms,

to microwave meals and pornography.
Who wouldn't romanticize something as banal
as loneliness, the occasional trick who never

spent the night? Only Calvinist concepts
like providence and grace can explain how
those imaginary moors and glens led to this:

waking wrapped in your body's mossy heath,
cats sprawled on the margins of our warmth.
While Bach dances up and down his crystal stairs,

you are filling omelettes with tarragon, prosciutto,
Gruyère, drizzling honey over English muffins.
Morning's remainder I lounge shirtless

and barefoot in the living room's long sun,
read Dante, listen to your laptop
tap. Winter wind outside is herding off

the sad leaves and rippling chilly treetops.
How simple, the symmetries of happiness.
No blood-red embellishments, no onyx arabesques.

Only heat-drowsy cats, rosemary plants.
And one shifting gift: to be sheeted in gold,
lying in the light as long as it lasts.

German Village

History has followed us here
across a galaxy of cold gray water.
Within the maples' October smolder,
staked heretics shriek in the town square,
books blacken along Unter den Linden,
the chimneys of Buchenwald sigh
their sooty breath. Even in heaven
we cannot forget conflagrations,
gathering up the bouquets of burning,
maple leaves we press to our faces,
breathing deep their fire.

This is the afterlife we want: a universe
of brick, extensions of every earthly
appetite, recompense for every suffered
sorrow. An immigrant dreams of density:
slate-roofed cottages, chimney pots,
embroidered lintels, limestone stoops.

And chrysanthemum dusk, a cold wind
curling our collars up. The saved
soon learn how simply blessing's bred:
brisk walks along brick streets and autumn air,
church spires spiked with moonlight.
Night harvests the brittle wings of bats,
rakes and rustles leaf-scattered streets.
Outside the brew pub's golden windows,
the darkness sharpens, waits and yearns.

Now our names are called, we enter in.
Angels appear with steins of lager,
platters of sauerkraut and wurst,
Kartoffelsalat mit Speck, cherry strudel
furbelowed with whipped cream and folk song.
Beneath the table you squeeze my thigh.

Tonight we will lie together beneath quilts,
warm and naked, watching hearth fire dwindle.
Long after midnight I will wake, close the flue,
curl against you, listening to heaven's dark breath,
hard wind shaking flame from maple boughs.

Helvetia

(for Eleanor Mailloux)

Miles from anywhere, that's the point,
where Swiss settlers, lost, settled down
in 1869. How to live with peace,

that's the problem, how to forget phones,
paper piles, meetings, computers, ambitions.
It takes a while, the way a body,

used to tension, is slow to relax
beneath the masseur's hard hands.
A small rain drips morning off the eaves,

off the long green fingers of spruce.
Snow drops lift from the earth their tiny
porcelain lanterns, a new year's light.

We stroll away the afternoon, speaking only
to bearded billy goats, muddy calves,
one squeaky cat hungry for a hand stroke,

a few white ducks on the trout stream's burble.
Dinner's in the Hutte Restaurant,
where Eleanor fries up rösti on the woodstove,

serves us the local sausage, cheese, history,
home-baked bread; sauerbraten, sauerkraut,
hill-country manners and hot peach cobbler.

Then a ring around the March moon,
and our room in the Beekeeper Inn,
reading till we're drowsy, then lying in

the dark, listening to church chimes
quarter the hours, the purl of the creek
constant, a quiet, comprehensible eternity.

Dueling Feasts

For months now, we have taken turns—
French onion soup with croutons and cheese;
Belgian endives wrapped in ham, topped
with Gruyère; eggs Benedict, chiles rellenos,

fried oysters, cream pies, martinis,
Manhattans, champagne—then separating
for solitary gym-work on treadmill, NordicTrack,
grateful for baggy sweater weather,

pinching fingerfuls of waist and whining.
Mid-January your best dress pants' button
pops off like a plastic meteorite, and then
you lay down the law—no alcohol on weekdays,

no dairy products, no second helpings,
no desserts. Barbed-wire disciplines,
the cattle chawing dry straw and staring
at verboten emerald lawns. God knows

neither of us can afford a new wardrobe,
and these jeans are tight enough.
But give me a lover with some surplus,
a few handfuls of furry belly I can pat

in the drowse on either side of sleep,
stroke as proof of appetite—its depth,
variety, the delights its sating inspires.
Distance the skeleton, bury it

in flesh. At least once a week,
allow my hunger joyful excess:
a wedge of Appenzeller cheese,
Greek olives, split-pea soup

with ham hocks, a few rich bites

of marzipan, celebrating these brief days
of abundance, our days and nights together.
Soon enough, the trash can tipped over

by starveling dogs, birds pecking
at shriveled winter's wild rose hips,
seed-scattered snow. Soon enough,
lichen's food, names etched in stone.

Bereft

Another of my nightmares shakes us both
awake. In that world where mist's

perennial, where one squints through
nearsighted gel, you leave me

in many ways. Amidst the usual theaters
of departure, by plane or train.

Or absurdly, donning a mask and snorkle,
striding into the waves. You leave,

and you do not return.
I have my petty keenery and complaint,

like any spouse: your love of shopping's
tedious, your laptop's ubiquitous, you are

not rough enough in bed. But when
the headlines smoke with fallen planes,

interstate gut trails, air running out
fifty fathoms down, suddenly I see

martini glasses hammered into shards,
your clothes boxed up, the garden

herbs uprooted one by one.
And in high school, that experiment:

bean seeds planted, then raised
in closet dark, just to see what pale

and twisted shapes they will take,
those lives bereft of light.

Two Glasses of Wine

You leave Charleston at five,
      your space-age office furniture, iMacs
      and plate-glass windows,
as I unpack the groceries, watch
The Simpsons, indulge in a shot of Scotch.

You're doing 70 along the Kanawha now,
      past Marmet's chemical factories
      with their flame-flaring towers,
some lemon-rosemary chicken
packed in a cooler in your trunk:
      for my freezer, for those nights
      alone when I don't want to cook.

Now I'm reconnoitering the recipes again,
      from *The Frugal Gourmet Cooks Three Ancient Cuisines,*
        and beginning the tedium of peeling shrimp.

You've slipped up Cabin Creek, where
      the West Virginia Turnpike slows to sixty,
where striking miners assembled
      almost a century ago.
$1.25 at the toll, then weaving
      around trucks and up the grade onto
        the Beckley plateau.

The feta needs crumbling,
the tomato sauce needs cinnamon,

while the highway slides between
      week-old snowbanks and groves of hemlock,
you crest Flat Top Mountain
and begin that long slope down, vistas
      of blue gray, the hills of Mercer County.

Greek village salad with cabbage:

the onions, peppers, olives, and feta must marinate
an hour, and I've forgotten to chill the Chardonnay.
The moon's up now, over the line of pines
in my backyard, over

what I call "The Dramatic Cleft," where 460
and the New River cut through Peter's Mountain,
the water runs white along rapids, and
you spy the lights of Narrows.

I'm watching the clock now,
heating water for the pasta,
wrapping olive bread in aluminum foil
to warm in the oven,
watching the clock. If all goes well,
you're due within half an hour,
in a world without rock slides,
drunken drivers and sleepy truckers,
imperfect machinery.

I wait for your headlights to appear
in my yard, beneath the old oak.

I wait to pour two glasses of wine.

Homecoming

Today, mid-November, my lover, my sister, and I,
we're carrying box after box of Ball jars to the basement,
riches my father has grown and canned. Lime pickles,
spaghetti sauce, green beans, tomatoes, strawberry jam.

Hinton, West Virginia, is much the same, that Appalachia
my teenaged years so wanted to escape. There's a storefront
preacher shouting about perversity, a bookish boy with a split lip.
There's a gang outside a Madam's Creek farmhouse shouting
"Come out here, you queers. We'll change you."

Now I know only five hours away, amidst DC traffic,
crowded sidewalks, men are holding hands along 17th Street,
buying gay novels in Lambda Rising, sipping Scotch
and flirting in the leather bars. But I want to be here,

in West Virginia,
where my ancestors worked their farms, where, today,
we form this assembly line from kitchen to basement.
John hands me a box of bread-and-butter pickles,
I lug it down the cellar stairs. There, amidst cobwebs,

Amy's lining up the jars, greens and reds,
with their masking-tape dates, joining other summers
packed away. I want to be here,
where first ice collects along the creeks,
where the mountains' fur turns pewter gray,
and my father mulches quiescent gardens with fallen leaves.

Early evening's hard rain, hill coves filling with mist.
After pinto beans, turnip greens, and corn bread,
John's drowsing on the couch, I'm fingerpicking
a little guitar by the fire. There on the coffee table,
gifts Amy's left for us: a jar of spaghetti sauce, a jar of jam.
There on the mantelpiece, my mother's urn.

The boy who fled Hinton twenty-five years ago,
he's here too, the boy who dreamed
of packed disco bars, summers on Fire Island,
fascinating city men, the boy who did not yet know
what family meant. His hair is thick and black,
his beard is sparse, still dark. He shakes his head,
amazed that I've come back willingly, even for
a weekend. An ember flares up, fingernails of freezing
rain tick the windows. The boy, bemused, studies
the lines on my brow, shyly strokes the silver in my beard.

CPSIA information can be obtained at www.ICGtesting.com
Printed in the USA
LVOW12s0312090714

393442LV00012B/338/P

9 780821 416501